高职高专土建系列规划教材
21世纪高职高专土建系列技能型规划教材

建筑工程专业英语

（第二版）

主　编　吴承霞　宋贵彩
副主编　宋　乔　吕秀娟　李　奎
参　编　尚瑞娟　许法轩　关永冰
　　　　赵　娜　宿翠霞
主　审　姜红艳

北京大学出版社
PEKING UNIVERSITY PRESS

内 容 简 介

本书的主要任务是使学生能够在学习大学英语及专业课的基础上,初步了解土建类专业英语的写作特点,掌握必备的土建类专业英语词汇及术语,基本上能够借助工具书阅读土建类专业英语文章,在一定程度上掌握土建类专业英语的翻译技巧,为更好地从事土建筑类专业的工作打下较扎实的基础。

本书以培养学生的专业英语阅读能力为主要目标,内容涉及:建筑工程概论、建筑工程制图识图与CAD基础、建筑材料、建筑构造、建筑工程测量、建筑结构、建筑施工、工程监理、建筑施工管理、建筑工程造价估算、绿色建筑、梁思成简介、BIM等多个方面。本书既注重讲解土建类专业英语的知识,又介绍了有关土建类的专业知识。

本书可作为高等职业院校土建类专业的教材,也可供土建类专业技术人员学习和参考使用。

图书在版编目(CIP)数据

建筑工程专业英语 / 吴承霞,宋贵彩主编. —2版. —北京:北京大学出版社,2016.2
(21世纪高职高专土建系列技能型规划教材)
ISBN 978-7-301-26597-0

Ⅰ. ①建… Ⅱ. ①吴…②宋… Ⅲ. ①建筑工程—英语—高等职业教育—教材 Ⅳ. ①H31

中国版本图书馆 CIP 数据核字(2015)第 293081 号

书　　　名	建筑工程专业英语(第二版) JIANZHU GONGCHENG ZHUANYE YINGYU
著作责任者	吴承霞　宋贵彩　主编
策划编辑	赖　青　杨星璐
责任编辑	杨星璐　商武瑞
标准书号	ISBN 978-7-301-26597-0
出版发行	北京大学出版社
地　　　址	北京市海淀区成府路 205 号　100871
网　　　址	http://www.pup.cn　新浪微博:@北京大学出版社
电子信箱	pup_6@163.com
电　　　话	邮购部 010-62752015　发行部 010-62750672　编辑部 010-62750667
印　刷　者	北京圣夫亚美印刷有限公司
经　销　者	新华书店
	787 毫米×1092 毫米　16 开本　10.5 印张　242 千字 2009 年 7 月第 1 版 2016 年 2 月第 2 版　2021 年 1 月第 4 次印刷(第总 15 次印刷)
定　　　价	24.00 元

未经许可,不得以任何方式复制或抄袭本书之部分或全部内容。
版权所有,侵权必究
举报电话:010-62752024　电子信箱:fd@pup.pku.edu.cn
图书如有印装质量问题,请与出版部联系,电话:010-62756370

第二版前言

随着我国改革开放步伐的进一步加快，涉外建筑工程项目越来越多，土建类高等职业院校的学生参与国际间的学术交流已不再是梦想，但要更好地了解和学习国外先进的建筑科学技术，看懂国外建筑工程图纸，学生必须具备一定的阅读土建类专业英语的能力和水平。

编者建议：土建类高等职业院校的学生在学习时，应更加注重阅读，通过阅读，学习了解专业英语的写作特点，掌握必备的土建类专业英语词汇及术语，掌握各篇课文所描述的相关专业知识，从而能够借助工具书阅读土建类专业英语文章，在一定程度上掌握土建类专业英语的翻译技巧。

本书以培养学生的专业英语阅读能力为主要目标，内容涉及：建筑工程概论、建筑工程制图识图与CAD基础、建筑材料、建筑构造、建筑工程测量、建筑结构、建筑施工、工程监理、建筑施工管理、建筑工程造价估算、绿色建筑、梁思成简介、BIM（建筑信息模型），基本涵盖了土建类专业所开设的课程内容。每一课包括课文（Text）、参考译文（Translation）和阅读材料（Reading Material）三部分。各篇课文是体现土建类专业英语特征的非科普性文章，阅读材料的选取则注重趣味性和科普性。每篇文章均给出了相应的专业词汇注解，其中各篇课文后面还对文中的疑难句进行了注释。本书最后还给出了建筑工程常用的名词、术语等。本书建议总学时为30学时。

本书由吴承霞和宋贵彩担任主编，宋乔、吕秀娟和李奎担任副主编，尚瑞娟、许法轩、关永冰、赵娜和宿翠霞参编，姜红艳任主审。具体编写分工如下：第1课、第4课由宋贵彩编写，第2课由宿翠霞编写，第3课由赵娜编写，第5课、第7课由吕秀娟编写，第6课、第11课由宋乔编写，第8课由许法轩编写，第9课由关永冰编写，第10课由尚瑞娟编写，第12课、第13课由李奎编写，阅读材料及附录由吴承霞编写。全书由吴承霞统稿，姜红艳主审。

本书第一版由吴承霞担任主编，袁学锋、赵娜、关永冰、宿翠霞和宋贵彩担任副主编，吕秀娟、宋乔、崔春霞和李奎参编。在此向第1版的各位编者表示诚挚的感谢！

由于编写水平有限，书中尚有不足之处，恳切希望读者批评指正。

编　者
2015年7月

第一版前言

随着我国改革开放步伐的进一步加快,涉外建筑工程项目越来越多,土建类高等职业学校的学生参与国际间的学术交流已不再是梦想,但要更好地了解和学习国外先进的建筑科学技术,看懂国外建筑工程图纸,学生必须具备一定的阅读土建类专业英语的能力和水平。

编者建议:土建类高等职业学校的学生在学习时,应更加注重阅读,通过学习了解专业英语的写作特点,掌握必备的土建类专业英语词汇及术语,掌握各课课文所描述的相关专业知识,从而能够借助工具书阅读土建类专业英语文章,在一定程度上掌握土建类专业英语的翻译技巧。

本书以培养学生的专业英语阅读能力为主要目标,内容涉及:建筑工程概论、建筑工程制图识图与CAD基础、建筑材料、建筑构造、建筑工程测量、建筑力学、建筑结构、建筑设备、建筑施工、建筑施工管理、建筑节能、梁思成简介,基本上涵盖了土建类专业所开设的课程内容。每一课包括课文(Text)、参考译文(Translation)和阅读材料(Reading material)三部分。各课课文是体现土建类专业英语特征的非科普性文章,阅读材料的选取则注重趣味性和科普性。每篇文章均给出了相应的专业词汇注解,其中各课课文后面还对文中的疑难句进行了注释。本书最后还给出了科技论文的阅读与写作以及建筑工程常用的名词、术语等。本书建议总学时为30学时。

全书由吴承霞统稿,第1课、第4课由宋贵彩编写,第2课由宿翠霞编写,第3课由赵娜编写,第5课、第9课由吕秀娟编写,第6课及附录A由崔春霞编写,第7课、第11课由宋乔编写,第8课由袁学锋编写,第10课由关永冰编写,第12课由李奎编写,第1课、第4课、第5课、第6课、第7课、第9课的阅读材料及附录B由吴承霞编写,其余阅读材料为该课的作者编写。

由于编写水平有限,书中尚有不足之处,恳切希望读者批评指正。

编　者

2009年5月

Lesson 1	Building Engineering	1
Lesson 2	The Architectural Charting Drawing Recognition and CAD	12
Lesson 3	Building Materials	22
Lesson 4	Building Components	31
Lesson 5	Building Engineering Surveying	42
Lesson 6	Building Structures	52
Lesson 7	Building Construction	65
Lesson 8	Engineering Construction Supervision	77
Lesson 9	Project Management	85
Lesson 10	Cost Estimation of Construction Project	95
Lesson 11	Green Building	105
Lesson 12	Profile: Liang Ssu-ch'eng	116
Lesson 13	Building Information Modeling (BIM)	129

附录A　NEW WORDS AND PHRASES　137
附录B　建筑工程常用术语翻译及名词解释　144
参考文献　158

Lesson 1　Building Engineering

Text

Types of buildings　A building is closely bound up with people, for it provides people with the necessary space to work and live in.

As classified by their use, buildings are mainly of two types: industrial buildings and civil buildings (Fig 1.1, Fig 1.2). Industrial buildings are used by various factories or industrial production while civil buildings are those that are used by people for dwelling, employment, education and other social activities[1].

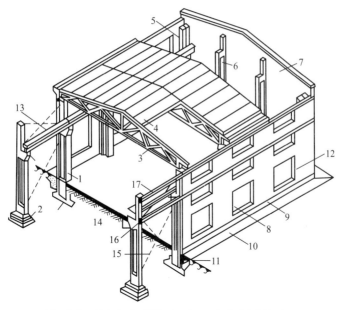

Fig 1.1　Fabricated Single-storey Industrial Factory

1—column; 2—foundation; 3—roof truss; 4—roof slab; 5—corner column;
6—wind resistant column; 7—gable wall; 8—windows; 9—plinth; 10—aprou;
11—foundation beam; 12—external longitudinal wall; 13—crane beam; 14—ground;
15—column bracing; 16—connecting beam; 17—ring beam

As classified by their structural types, buildings are mainly of four types: frame structures (Fig 1.3) where a frame, or skeleton, holds up the weight and other materials are used to close the building up; mass wall structures (Fig 1.4), where solid materials such as brick, concrete and other types of masonry are used to build heavy walls that hold up the building; mixed bearing structure is composed of frame structure and bearing wall supporting all the weight together; space structure formed by reinforced concrete and steel support the loads, for example, truss structure, cable structure, shell structure etc..

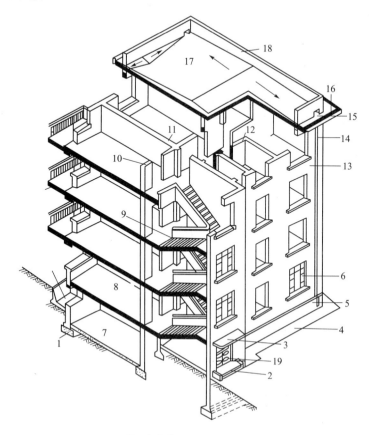

Fig 1.2 A Civil Building

1—foundation; 2—step; 3—canopy; 4—scatter water; 5—plinth; 6—window; 7—basement; 8—floor; 9—stairs; 10—internal longitudinal wall; 11—internal transverse wall; 12—partition; 13—external wall; 14—drainpipe; 15—water outlet; 16—overhang eaves; 17—roof; 18—parapet; 19—door

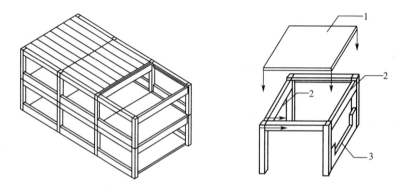

Fig 1.3 Frame Structures

1—slab; 2—main beam; 3—filler wall

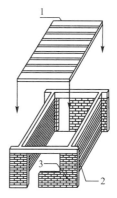

Fig 1. 4　Mass Wall Structure
1—prefabricated slab; 2—bearing wall; 3—self-supporting wall

As classified by their materials of the load-carrying frame, buildings are mainly of types: wood structure, masonry structure, reinforced concrete structure, steel structure and mixed structure.

Structure of buildings　Considering only the engineering essentials, the structure of a building can be defined as the assemblage of those parts which exist for the purpose of maintaining shape and stability. Its primary purpose is to resist any loads applied to the building and to transmit those to the ground[2].

Structural members　Structure of buildings is combined with various structural members, such as beams, columns, floors, walls, trusses.

A bar that is subjected to forces acting vertically its axis is called a beam. A beam is a typically flexural member and frequently encountered in structures. We will consider only a few of the simplest types of beams, such as those shown in Fig 1. 5.

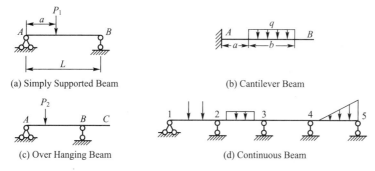

Fig 1. 5　Types of Beams

Columns are vertical compression members of a structural frame intended to support the load-carrying beams. They transmit loads from the upper floors to the lower levels and then to the soil through the foundations. We will consider a few of types of columns, such as those shown in Fig 1.6.

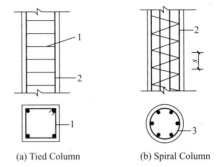

(a) Tied Column　　(b) Spiral Column

1—transverse ties stirrup, 2—longitudinal steel bar, 3—spiral stirrup

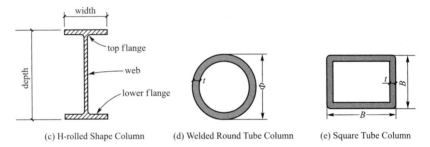

(c) H-rolled Shape Column　　(d) Welded Round Tube Column　　(e) Square Tube Column

Fig 1.6　Types of Columns

Plane truss (Fig 1.7) is composed by a group of bars arranged in a triangle on a plane.

(a) Parallel Truss　　(b) Nonparallel Truss

Fig 1.7　Plane Truss

Construction of buildings　Construction engineering is a specialized branch of civil engineering concerned with the planning, execution, and control of construction operations for various projects. Planning consists of scheduling the work to be done and selecting the most suitable construction methods and equipment for the project. Execution requires the timely mobilization of all drawings, layouts, and materials on the job to prevent delays to the work. Control consists analyzing progress and cost to ensure that the project will be done on schedule and within the estimated cost.

Construction operations are generally classified according to specialized fields. These include preparation of the project site, earthmoving, foundation treatment, construction of load-carrying frame and electrical and mechanical installations.

However, the relative importance of each field is not the same in all cases[3].

New Words and Phrases

1. classify   [ˈklæsɪfaɪ]   分类
2. dwell   [dwel]   居住
3. frame   [freɪm]   框架
4. masonry   [ˈmeɪsənri]   砌体
5. truss   [trʌs]   桁架
6. shell   [ʃel]   壳体
7. cable   [ˈkeɪbl]   悬索
8. stability   [stəˈbɪləti]   稳定性
9. flexural   [ˈflekʃʊrəl]   弯曲的
10. axis   [ˈæksɪs]   轴向的
11. beam   [biːm]   梁
12. column   [ˈkɒləm]   柱
13. floor   [flɔː]   楼板
14. stirrup   [ˈstɪrəp]   箍筋
15. spiral   [ˈspaɪrəl]   螺旋形的
16. triangle   [ˈtraɪæŋgl]   三角形
17. execution   [eksɪˈkjuːʃn]   实施
18. layout   [ˈleɪaʊt]   布置

Notes

[1] Industrial buildings are used by various factories or industrial production while civil buildings are those that are used by people for dwelling, employment, education and other social activities.

工业建筑用于各种工厂或工业生产，而民用建筑指的是那些人们用以居住、工作、教育或进行其他社会活动的场所。

[2] Considering only the engineering essentials, the structure of a building can be defined as the assemblage of those parts which exist for the purpose of maintaining shape and stability. Its primary purpose is to resist any loads applied to the building and to transmit those to the ground.

建筑结构可定义为以保持形状和稳定为目的的各个基本构件的组合体。其基本目的是抵抗作用在建筑物上的各种荷载并把它传到地基上。

[3] Construction operations are generally classified according to specialized fields. These include preparation of the project site, earthmoving, foundation treatment, construction of load-carrying frame and electrical and mechanical installations. However, the relative importance of each field is not the same in all cases.

施工程序通常根据工种不同来分类，包括现场准备、挖运土方、地基处理、主体结构施工以及电气和机械安装，但是每个工种的相对重要性在各种情况下并不总是相同的。

参 考 译 文

第1课 建筑工程概论

建筑物类型 建筑物与人类有着密切的关系，它能为人们的工作和生活提供必要的空间。

根据用途不同，可以将建筑物分为两大类：工业建筑和民用建筑（图1.1、图1.2），工业建筑用于各种工厂或工业生产，而民用建筑指的是那些人们用以居住、工作、教育或进行其他社会活动的场所。

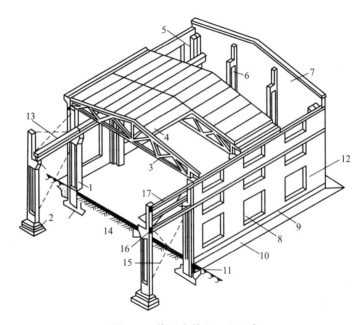

图 1.1 装配式单层工业厂房

1—柱子；2—基础；3—屋架；4—屋面板；5—角柱；6—抗风柱；7—山墙；
8—窗洞；9—勒脚；10—散水；11—基础梁；12—外纵墙；13—吊车梁；
14—地面；15—柱间支撑；16—连系梁；17—圈梁

根据结构形式的不同，建筑主要有四种类型：框架结构（图1.3），由框架（或称骨架）支承重量，同时用其他材料将建筑物围护起来；墙体承重结构（图1.4），用砖、砌块、混凝土建造墙体，由墙体支承建筑物；混合承重结构，由框架结构和墙体共同支撑重量；空间结构，由钢筋混凝土或钢组成空间结构支承重量，如网架、悬索、壳体等。

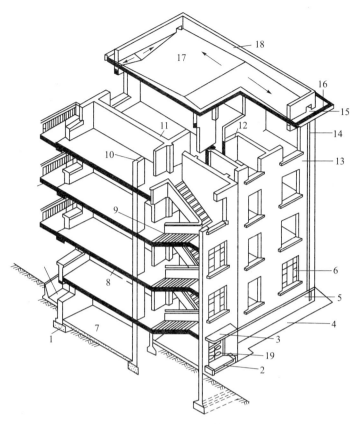

图 1.2 民用建筑
1—基础；2—台阶；3—雨篷；4—散水；5—勒脚；6—窗；7—地下室；8—楼板；
9—楼梯；10—内纵墙；11—内横墙；12—隔墙；13—外墙；14—落水管；
15—雨水口；16—挑檐沟；17—屋顶；18—女儿墙；19—门

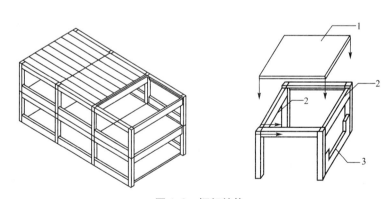

图 1.3 框架结构
1—楼板；2—主梁；3—填充墙

根据其主要承重构件所采用的材料不同，建筑物又分为木结构、砌体结构、钢筋混凝土结构、钢结构以及混合结构。

建筑结构 建筑结构可定义为以保持形状和稳定性为目的的各个基本构件的组合体。其基本目的是抵抗作用在建筑物上的各种荷载并把它传到地基上。

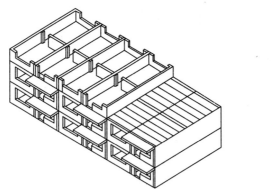
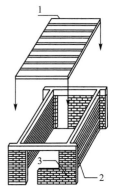

图 1.4 墙体承重结构

1—预制板；2—承重墙；3—自承重墙

结构构件 所有建筑物的结构都是由各种结构部件组合而成的，常见的有梁、板、柱、墙体、桁架等。

当一个杆件所受的力垂直于其轴线时，这样的杆件称为梁。梁是典型的受弯构件，而且常见于各种结构中。几种最简单的梁如图1.5所示。

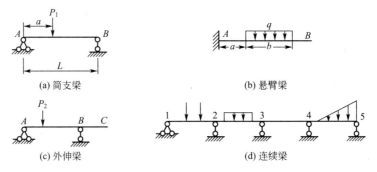

图 1.5 梁的类型

在框架结构中，柱是被用来支撑承重梁的竖向受压构件，上层楼板的荷载通过柱传到下层，然后经过基础传到土壤中。几种类型的柱如图1.6所示。

平面桁架(图1.7)是由排列在一个平面上的一组三角形构成的杆系结构。

建筑物的建造 建筑工程是土木工程的一个分支，涉及项目的计划、实施和施工控制。计划包括安排项目工作进程，选择适当的施工方法和设备。实施则要求及时筹备所有的图纸、布置和施工原料以防工作延期。控制包括进度和成本分析，以保证项目能按计划进行，并控制成本消耗在预期范围内。

施工程序通常根据工种不同来分类，包括现场准备、挖运土方、地基处理、主体结构施工以及电气和机械安装，但是每个工种的相对重要性在各种情况下并不总是相同的。

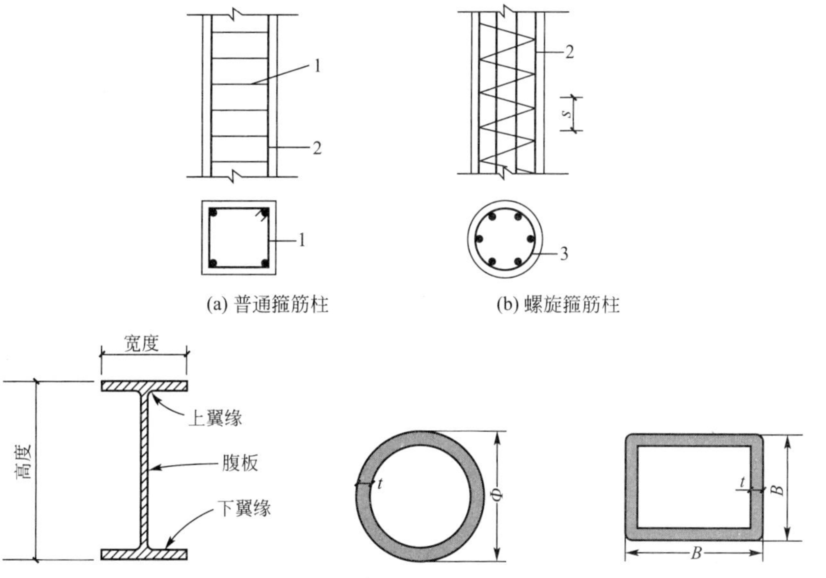

(a) 普通箍筋柱　　(b) 螺旋箍筋柱

(c) H形钢柱　　(d) 圆形钢管柱　　(e) 方形钢管柱

图 1.6　柱的类型

1—普通箍筋；2—纵筋；3—螺旋箍筋

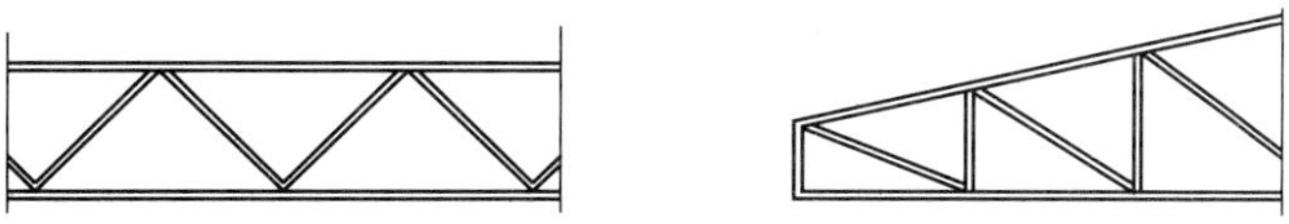

(a) 平行桁架　　(b) 不平行桁架

图 1.7　平面桁架

Reading material Ⅰ

Housing Problem in Big Cities

One problem that people in cities have is to find a comfortable place to live in. Land in cities is costly（昂贵的）, and every family cannot have a house of its own. Many poor people have to live in tenements（租金便宜的公寓）. A tenement is a large building with many rooms. The rooms do not have enough windows to let in light and fresh air. Tenements are often made of wood, and they catch fire easily. Poor people usually cannot afford more than two rooms for a family.

Whole sections of some cities are made up of tenements. Here, thousands of people live close together. Disease spreads easily. Children have to play on dangerous streets. These sections are usually called slums（贫民区）.

Apartment buildings that are roomier（宽敞的）and safer are made possible by new building materials. These materials are made in factories. One of them is reinforced concrete（钢筋混凝土）. It is concrete that contains steel rods to make it extra strong.

Steel is used to make a strong framework (框架) to hold (支撑) the floors and the roofs of the building. Reinforced concrete and steel make it possible to have buildings higher than ever before.

Elevators also help to make higher buildings possible. For many people, walking up and down many flights (梯段) of stairs would be difficult.

The hotel is another kind of building in cities. Large hotels are built partly because there are many salesmen (推销员) who travel regularly from city to city to sell goods from factories. Hotels provide comfortable places for them to stay. Still another kind of building is the office building. These are built for companies that want offices near the center of a large city.

Tall office buildings are usually called skyscrapers. The first skyscraper was built in Chicago, in 1885 and it had ten stories. The first skyscraper in New York was completed in 1902. Later, more and higher skyscrapers were built in New York, Chicago, and many other big cities all over the world.

Reading material II

Beijing, the Capital of the People's Republic of China

Beijing, the capital of the People's Republic of China, lies in North China. It is a city famous in the world. It has a history over three thousand years and a splendid (辉煌的) heritage (文化遗产) of ancient culture. The city and its surroundings are rich in scenic beauty. Today, as China's political, economic and cultural centre, Beijing further attracts the attention of the people across the world.

The famous May 4th Movement against imperialism (帝国主义) and feudalism (封建主义) started in Beijing in 1919. It marked the beginning of China's new-democratic movement. Beijing entered upon a new life in January 1949 when the city was liberated. On October 1st that year, Chairman Mao proclaimed from Tian An Men to the world the founding of the People's Republic of China.

The grand ancient buildings of old Beijing show fully the wisdom (智慧) of the laboring people who built the city, the Heaven Temple, the Forbidden City, the Summer Palace, just to cite a few. Since 1949, construction has been going on in all directions. Grand buildings sprang up one after another. The People's Great Hall, for example, was completed within a matter of ten months. As the open-to-the-outside-world policies have been carried out since the 1980s, more efforts have been made to make the city more beautiful. Every day Beijing is visited by hundreds of thousands of people from abroad.

Beijing takes on a new look. One can see the city is throbbing (跳动) with a vigorous (有活力的) life, which makes Beijing ever so young and ever so grand.

Lesson 2 The Architectural Charting Drawing Recognition and CAD

Text

1. The Architectural Charting and Drawing Recognition

The architectural engineering plat is one kind of the engineering plat, which is used to express the shape, size, material, structure, construction mode of the building as well as the specification and so on[1]. It is not only an important tool to express design intentions, exchange technology thoughts, but also an important technical document to instruct technical work such as production, construction, management and so on.

1) Projection charting

The concept of projection The projection phenomenon refers to that if an object is irradiated under the sunlight or lamplight, it will leave a shadow on the ground or on the wall. By scientifically and abstractly summarizing the relationship between object and shadow in the long-term production practice, people sum up the method of projection. The projection is widely used to express the object in the engineering circle, so as to realize the interconversion between three-dimensional objects and two-dimensional objects.

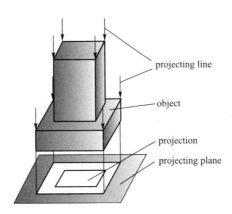

Fig 2.1 Projecting Process

Three basic elements that the projection must have are the projection line, the object, the projecting plane (Fig 2.1).

Projections commonly used in the project are three-plane projection drawing, the axonometric drawing and the perspective drawing (Fig 2.2).

Three-plane projection drawing Three-plane projection drawing is the main pattern in the project, which can accurately reflect the shape and size of object and is convenient to chat[2]. In the ordinary circumstances, three-plane projection drawing is composed of the horizontal projection drawing, the frontal projection drawing and the profile projection drawing. In the analysis

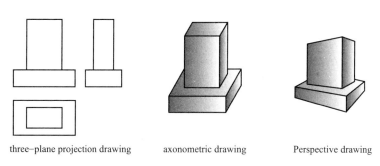

Fig 2.2 Projection

process of three-plane projection drawing, we are required to follow the projection relation of "equality in height, width and length", which is the foundation of drawing and reading.

2) The reading of architectural drawing

Fig 2.3 is a building, Fig 2.4 is it's horizontal plane, Fig 2.5 is south elevation and Fig 2.6 is the section.

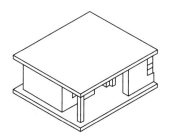

Fig 2.3 The Perspective Drawing

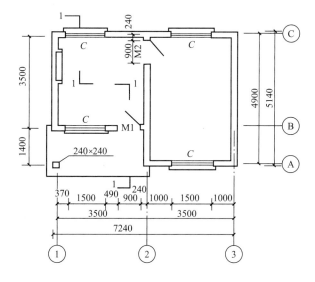

Fig 2.4 House Horizontal Plane

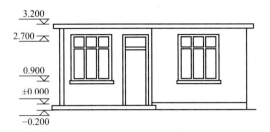

Fig 2.5 South Elevation

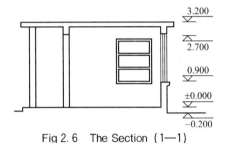

Fig 2.6 The Section (1—1)

2. Computer Aided Design (CAD)

1) What is CAD

CAD is an acronym for Computer Aided Design or Drafting. CAD program/software is an electronic tool that enables you to make quick and accurate drawings with the use of a computer. Computer drawings are neat, clean, highly presentable, and can be modified easily. With CAD, parts or components can be modeled, visualized, revised, and improve on the computer screen before any engineering drawings have been created. Now, we understand the CAD graphics interface (Fig2.7).

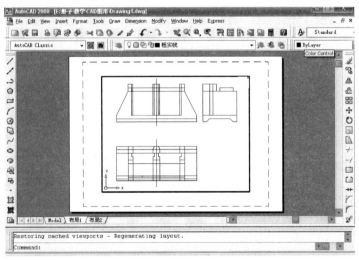

Fig 2.7 The CAD Graphics Interface

2) Capabilities of CAD

• Presentations

—You can create fine drawings with presentation symbols and text styles.

—You can use CAD program to make on screen presentations.

• Flexibility in editing

—CAD provides the flexibility to make quick alterations to drawings

—Some of the editing capabilities are such as move or copy drawing elements, enlarge or reduce size of a drawing, make multiple copies of a drawing, change units of measure and etc.

• Units and accuracy level

—CAD program allows you to work with great accuracy. You can also work with different units of measure, such as architectural units, engineering units, scientific units and surveyor units.

• Storage and access of drawings

—It is quick and convenient to organize CAD drawings. You can have thousands of drawings on a computer's hard disk and you can open any one of them within seconds.

• Sharing CAD drawings

—The drawings can be shared by a number of users, allowing them to coordinate projects and work as a team. This is accomplished by connecting different computers via a network. You can also publish your drawings on the Internet and collaborate CAD projects using a web site.

New Words and Phrases

1.	architectural	[ˌɑːkɪˈtektʃərəl]	建筑；建筑学的
2.	engineering	[ˌendʒɪˈnɪərɪŋ]	工程；工程的
3.	chart	[tʃɑːt]	图，图表；绘图，制图
4.	structure	[ˈstrʌktʃə]	结构，构造
5.	construction	[kənˈstrʌkʃn]	建设，施工
6.	curriculum	[kəˈrɪkjələm]	课程
7.	projection	[prəˈdʒekʃn]	投影
8.	three-dimensional	[ˌθriːdɪˈmenʃənəl]	三维的
9.	interconversion	[ˌɪntəkənˈvɜːʒən]	相互转换
10.	horizontal	[ˌhɒrɪzɒntl]	水平面；水平的
11.	frontal	[ˌfrʌntl]	房屋正面；正面的
12.	profile	[ˈprəʊfaɪl]	侧面，剖面
13.	section	[ˈsekʃn]	剖面
14.	acronym	[ˈækrənɪm]	缩写词

Notes

[1] The architectural engineering plat is one kind of the engineering plat, which is used to express the shape, size, material, structure, construction mode of the building as well as the specification and so on.

建筑工程图是工程图中的一种,用来表达建筑物的形状、大小、材料、结构、构造方式以及技术要求等。

[2] Three-plane projection drawing is the main pattern in the project, which can accurately reflect the shape and size of object and is convenient to chat.

三面投影图是工程上最主要的图样,其优点是能够准确地反映物体的形状和大小,作图方便。

参 考 译 文

第2课 建筑工程制图识图与CAD基础

1. 建筑工程制图与识图

建筑工程图是工程图中的一种,用来表达建筑物的形状、大小、材料、结构、构造方式以及技术要求等。它是表达设计意图、交流技术思想的重要工具,也是指导生产、施工、管理等技术工作的重要技术文件。

1) 投影制图

投影的概念 物体在阳光或灯光的照射下,在地面或墙面上会产生影子,这就是投影现象。人们在长期的生产实践中,将物体与影子之间的关系进行科学的、抽象的总结,从而归纳出投影法。在工程界中广泛采用投影的方法表达物体,以实现三维物体与二维物体的相互转换。

产生投影必须具备的3个基本要素是投射线、物体、投影面(图2.1)。

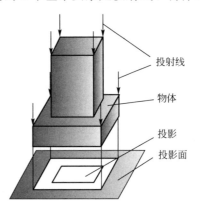

图2.1 投影过程

工程中常用的投影图有三面投影图、轴测图和透视图(图 2.2)。

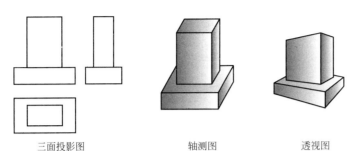

三面投影图　　轴测图　　透视图

图 2.2　投影

三面投影图　三面投影图是工程上最主要的图样,其优点是能够准确地反映物体的形状和大小,作图方便。在一般情况下,三面投影图由水平投影图、正面投影图、侧面投影图组成。在三面投影图的分析过程中,应遵循"长对正、高平齐、宽相等"的投影关系,它是绘图和识图的基础。

2)建筑图识读

如图 2.3 所示是一幢建筑物,图 2.4 为其平面图,图 2.5 为其南立面图,图 2.6 为 1—1 剖面图。

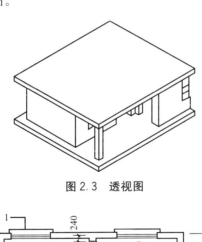

图 2.3　透视图

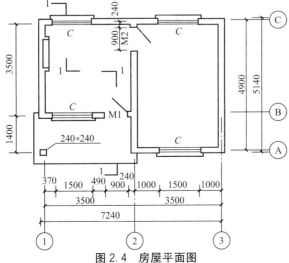

图 2.4　房屋平面图

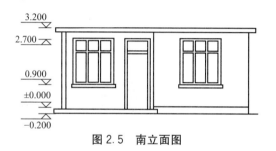

图 2.5　南立面图

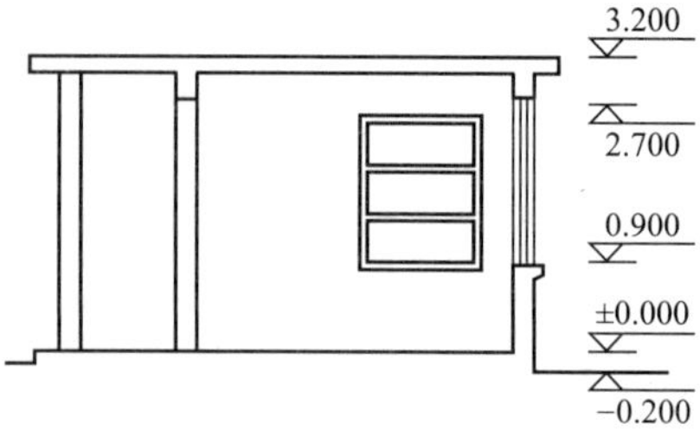

图 2.6　1—1 剖面图

2. 计算机辅助设计（CAD）

1) 什么是 CAD

CAD 是计算机辅助设计或绘图的简称。CAD 程序/软件是一种电子工具，用一台电脑就能够快速和准确地绘制图纸。其绘制的图纸整洁、干净、非常漂亮，且容易被修改。CAD 可以将零部件或构件建模、可视化、修改，而且可以在电脑屏幕上改进以前已经创建的任何工程图纸。现在来认识一下 CAD 的绘图界面，如图 2.7 所示。

2) CAD 的功能

• 演示

——可以创建具有良好图像符号和文本样式的图纸；

——可以在屏幕上演示 CAD 程序。

• 灵活的编辑

——CAD 可以灵活、快速地修改图纸；

——编辑功能，如移动或复制绘图单元，放大或缩小绘图的尺寸，重复拷贝图纸，计量单位变化等。

• 模块化和精度

——CAD 能提高绘图的准确性。还可以用不同的模块，如建筑模块，工程模块，科学单位和测量单元。

• 图纸的存储和取用

——能快速、方便地编组 CAD 图纸。可以有成千上万的图纸在计算机的硬盘上，并且可以在几秒钟内打开它们中的任何一个。

• 共享 CAD 图纸

——计算机通过网络连接起来，能使一个合作项目团队的用户共享图纸。也可以用网站在互联网上发布图纸以协作同一个 CAD 项目。

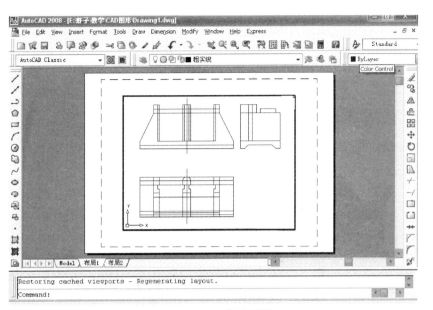

图 2.7　CAD 绘图界面

Reading material Ⅰ

Architectural Drawing

From his appearance on earth to the end of his cave-dwelling days, man had very little need for architectural drawing. When man for the most part abandoned cave dwelling, cave-like shelters appeared. They were simple in design and their construction matched the technology of that day. Drawing was not necessary. The appearance of formal shapes with remarkably accurate dimensions（非常精确的尺寸）, however, suggests there was a need for architectural drawing. It is difficult to imagine achieving such precision（准确的）work with the limited construction technology available without some form of pictorial（绘图）planning and documentation（文档）.

With more complex building being built, it became necessary to develop more elaborate（复杂的）drawing methods. In the last few hundred years, architectural drawing has evolved into several general types. These range from concept sketches （草图）to intricate（精细的）details drawn to scale. Design sketches are rough drawing that are used as "idea sketches", made to explore concepts that will be refined at a later date. They may appear crude（粗糙的）to the casual（随意的）observer, but a closer study of sketches drawn by talented designers will usually reveal a theme and sensitivity containing the elements of good design. It is the purpose of these drawings to establish such elements. Design sketches have changed very little from the earliest known examples to those of today's architects.

The two pictures' comparison shows the development of simple building to complex building.

Simple Building

Complex Building

Reading material II

Cambridge, a University Town

When we say that Cambridge is a university town, we do not mean just that it is a town with a university in it. Manchester (曼彻斯特-英国英格兰西北部港市) and Milan (米兰) have universities. But we do not call them university towns. A university town is one where there is no clear separation between the university buildings and the rest of the city. The university is not just one part of the town, but it is all over the town. The heart of Cambridge has its shops, pubs, market places and so on, but most of it is university—colleges, faculties, libraries, clubs and other places for university staff and students. Students fill the shops, cafes, banks and churches, making these as well part of the university.

The town was there first. Two Romans crossed there, and there were signs of building before Roman times (earlier than 43A.D.). In 1226, the authority of the university, the chancellor (校长), was recognized by the king, and Cambridge became a centre of learning.

At that time many of the students were too poor to afford lodgings. Colleges were opened so that students could live cheaply. This was the beginning of the college system which has continued at Cambridge up to the present day.

The colleges were built with money from kings, queens, religious (宗教的) houses or other sources. One example is Clare College (克莱尔学院). It was first founded in 1326 as University Hall after the Black Death (a disease which killed half the population of England between 1349 and 1350). It was rebuilt with money from the countess of Clare. Today there are nearly thirty colleges. The newest are University College, founded in 1965, and Clare Hall, founded in 1966, both for graduates.

With about 8,250 undergraduates (本科生) and over 2,000 postgraduates (研究生), the city is a busy place in full term. Undergraduates are not allowed to keep cars in Cambridge, so nearly all of them use bicycles. Don't try to drive through Cambridge during the five minutes between lectures (课堂). If one has a lecture in Downing College at 9:55 and another in Trinity at 10, his bicycle must get him there through a boiling sea of other bicycles hurrying in all directions. If you are in Cambridge at five minutes to the hour any morning of full term, you will know that you are in a university town. Stop in some safe place, and wait.

Lesson 3 Building Materials

Text

Masonry   Masonry consists of natural materials, such as stone or manufactured products, such as brick and concrete blocks (Fig 3.1). Masonry has been used since ancient times: mud bricks were used in the city of Babylon for secular buildings, and stone was used for the great temples of the Nile Valley. The Great Pyramid in Egypt, standing 481 feet (147 meters) high, is the most spectacular masonry construction. Masonry units originally were stacked without using any bonding agent, but all modern masonry construction uses a cement mortar as a bonding material. Modern structural materials include stones, bricks and concrete blocks.

Fig 3.1 Masonry

Timber   Timber is one of the earliest construction materials and one of the few natural materials with good tensile properties. Hundreds of different species of wood are found throughout the world, and each species exhibits different physical characteristics.

Because of the cellular nature of wood, it is stronger along the grain than across the grain. Wood is particularly strong in tension and compression parallel to the grain, and it has great bending strength. These properties make it ideally suited for columns and beams in structures (Fig 3.2). Wood is not effectively used as a tensile member in a truss, however, because the tensile strength of a truss member depends upon connections between members.

Steel   Steel is an outstanding structural material (Fig 3.3). It has a high strength on a pound-for-pound basis when compared to other materials, even though its volume-for-volume weight is more than ten times that of wood. It has a high elastic modulus, which results in small deformations under load. It can be formed by rolling into various structural shapes such as I-beams, plates, and sheets; it also can be cast into complex shapes; and it is also produced in the form of wire strands and ropes for use as cables in suspension bridges and suspended roofs, as elevator ropes, and as wires for prestressed concrete. Steel elements can be joined together by various means, such as bolting, riveting, or welding. Carbon steels are subject to corrosion through oxidation and must be protected from contact with the atmosphere by painting them or embedding them in concrete. Above temperature of about 371℃, steel rapidly loses its strength, and therefore it must be covered in a jacket of a fireproof material to increase its fire resistance.

Fig 3.2 Timber   Fig 3.3 Steel

Concrete Concrete is a mixture of water, sand and gravel, and Portland cement (Fig 3.4). Crushed stone, manufactured lightweight stone, and seashells are often used in lieu of natural gravel. Portland cement, which is a mixture of materials containing calcium and clay, is heated in a kiln and then pulverized. Concrete derives its strength from the fact that pulverized Portland cement, when mixed with water, hardens by a process called hydration. In an ideal mixture, concrete consists of about three fourths sand and gravel (aggregate) by volume and one fourth cement paste. The physical properties of concrete are highly sensitive to variations in the mixture of the components, so a particular combination of these ingredients must be custom-designed to achieve specified results in terms of strength or shrinkage. When concrete is poured into a mold or form, it contains free water, not required for hydration, which evaporates. As the concrete hardens, it releases this excess water over a period of time and shrinks. As a result of this shrinkage, fine cracks often develop. In order to minimize these shrinkage cracks, concrete must be hardened by keeping it moist for at least 5 days. The strength of concrete increases in time because the hydration process continues for years; as a practical matter, the strength at 28 days is considered standard.

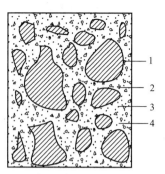

Fig 3.4　Concrete
1—gravel; 2—sand; 3—cement paste; 4—pore

Concrete deforms under load in an elastic manner. Although its elastic modulus is one tenth that of steel, similar deformations will result since its strength is also about one tenth that of steel. Concrete is basically a compressive material and has negligible tensile strength.

Reinforced concrete　Reinforced concrete has steel bars that are placed in a concrete member to carry tensile forces. These reinforced bars have wrinkles on the surfaces to ensure a bond with the concrete. Although reinforced concrete was developed in many countries, its discovery is usually attributed to Joseph Monnier, a French gardener, who used a wire network to reinforce concrete tubes in 1868. This process is workable because steel and concrete expand and contract equally when the temperature changes. If this were not the case, the bond between the steel and concrete would be broken by a change in temperature since the two materials would respond differently. Reinforced concrete can be molded into innumerable shapes, such as beams, columns, slabs, and arches, and is therefore easily adapted to a particular form of building[1] (Fig 3.5).

Fig 3.5　Reinforced Concrete

New Words and Phrases

1. grain   [greɪn]   纹理
2. sheet   [ʃi:t]   薄板
3. bolt   [bəʊlt]   螺栓连接
4. rivet   [ˈrɪvɪt]   铆接
5. weld   [weld]   焊接
6. ductile   [ˈdʌktaɪl]   易变形的
7. extrude   [ɪkˈstru:d]   挤压成形
8. crush   [krʌʃ]   压碎
9. calcium   [ˈkælsɪəm]   钙
10. clay   [kleɪ]   黏土
11. kiln   [kɪln]   (用来烧或烘干砖等的)窑，炉
12. pulverize   [ˈpʌlvəraɪz]   使成粉末；研磨
13. ingredient [ɪnˈgri:dɪənt] 骨料
14. shrinkage   [ˈʃrɪŋkɪdʒ]   收缩
15. hydration   [haɪˈdreɪʃn]   水化作用
16. evaporate   [ɪˈvæpəreɪt]   蒸发，挥发
17. fine crack [faɪn kræk]   微裂缝
18. negligible [ˈneglɪdʒəbl]   可以忽略的；无关紧要的；微不足道的
19. bond   [bɒnd]   黏结

Notes

[1] Reinforced concrete can be molded into innumerable shapes, such as beams, columns, slabs, and arches, and is therefore easily adapted to a particular form of building.

钢筋混凝土可以浇注成各种形状，如梁、柱、板和拱，因而适用于特殊形态的建筑物中。

参考译文

第3课 建筑材料

砌体材料 砌体材料包括天然材料，比如石块，也包括人造产品，比如砖和混凝土砌块(图3.1)。古代人们就开始使用砌块了：巴比伦城中非宗教性质的建筑物就是用泥土烧制的砖建造的，尼罗河峡谷中的大庙宇是用石头建造的，高达481英尺(147米)的埃及金字塔是最壮观的砌体结构。最初砌块被堆叠到一起时不需要黏结剂，而现在所有的砌体结构都用水泥砂浆作为黏结材料。现代砌体材料包括石材、砖和混凝土砌块。

图 3.1　砌体材料

木材　木材是最早的结构材料之一,也是少有的几种具有较好抗拉性能的天然材料之一。全世界有数百种木材,每一种类都有不同的物理特性。

由于木材细胞组成的特点,木材沿着纹理方向的强度比垂直于纹理方向的大。平行于纹理方向的抗拉和抗压强度均较大,并且有很强的抗弯强度。这些特点使木材非常适合做结构中的柱子和梁(图3.2)。但是,木材并不适合做桁架中的抗拉杆件,因为桁架杆件的抗拉强度取决于杆件之间的连接。

钢材　钢材是一种重要的建筑材料(图3.3)。与其他材料相比,钢材的比重超过木材的10倍,其强度也远远高于其他材料。钢材的弹性模量很大,这使得钢材在荷载作用下变形较小。钢材可被轧制成各种各样的形状,像工字型梁,钢板;也可以浇注成一些复杂的形状;可以制成钢丝绳和钢丝索,用作悬索桥和悬挂屋面的钢缆,用作电梯缆索和预应力混凝土中的钢筋。钢构件的各部分可以通过多种方法连接起来,如螺栓连接、铆接或焊接。碳素钢在氧化作用下易被腐蚀,因此必须通过在其表面涂刷防锈漆或埋入混凝土中来避免与空气接触。当温度超过371℃时,钢材会迅速丧失强度,所以必须在钢材的表面做一层耐火材料来提高它的耐火性。

图 3.2　木材　　　　　　　　图 3.3　钢材

混凝土　混凝土是水、砂和砾石及波特兰水泥的混合物(图3.4)。碎石、人造轻骨料、贝壳经常被用来代替天然石料。波特兰水泥是将含有钙质材料和黏土的混合物在窑内进行煅烧,然后再研磨成粉末而形成的。混凝土的强度是通过将粉末状的波特兰水泥与水混合,经过水化作用并最终硬化而得到的。在理想的混合状态下,混凝土由占其体积大约3/4的砂、石子(骨料)和占其体积 1/4 的水泥浆组成。混凝土的物理特性对其混合物中成分的变化是极其敏感的，所以为了获得混凝土在强度和收缩等方面的特定效果，必须对这些组成材料的配料进行特定的设计。当往模具或模板中浇注时，混凝土中含有大量并非用于水化而是要蒸发掉的水。当混凝土硬化时，经过一段时间将蒸发掉多余的水而产生收缩，这种收缩通常将导致微裂缝的发展。为了减少这种收缩裂痕，混凝土的硬化必须保持在潮湿环境中至少 5 天。因此，由于混凝土的水化会维持多年，混凝土的强度随时间逐渐增长，事实上，常把混凝土养护 28 天的强度作为标准强度。

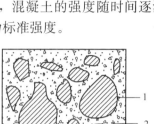

图 3.4　混凝土
1—石子；2—砂子；3—水泥浆；4—气孔

混凝土在荷载下会发生弹性变形。尽管它的弹性模量是钢材的 1/10，但由于它的强度大约也是钢材的 1/10，所以也可能发生相似的变形。混凝土主要用作抗压材料，其抗拉强度几乎可以忽略。

钢筋混凝土　钢筋混凝土构体中配有钢筋，用以承受拉力，其表面带肋，以保证与混凝土的黏结。尽管钢筋混凝土在很多国家得到发展，但其发明通常归功于约瑟夫·盟约，一位法国园丁，他在 1868 年曾使用钢筋网来加强混凝土管。由于温度变化时，钢材与混凝土胀缩系数相同，因此这种做法是可行的。如若不然，钢筋与混凝土之间的黏结会因温度的变化导致两者变形不一致而被破坏。钢筋混凝土可以浇注成各种形状，如梁、柱、板和拱，因而适用于特殊形态的建筑物中(图 3.5)。

图 3.5　钢筋混凝土

Reading material Ⅰ

Reinforcing Steels (钢筋) for Concrete

Compared with concrete, steel is a high strength material. The useful strength of ordinary reinforcing steels in tension as well as compression, i.e., the yield strength, is about fifteen times the compressive strength of common structural concrete, and well over one hundred times its tensile strength. On the other hand, steel is a high cost material compared with concrete. It follows that the two materials are best used in combination if the concrete is made to resist the compressive stresses and the compressive force, longitudinal (纵向的) steel reinforcing bars are located close to the tension face to resist the tension force, and usually additional steel bars are so disposed that they resist the inclined tension stresses that are caused by the shear force in the beams. However, reinforcement is also used for resisting compressive force primarily where it is desired to reduce the cross-sectional dimensions (尺寸) of compression members, as in the lower floor columns of multistory buildings (多层建筑). Even if no such necessity exists, a minimum amount of reinforcement is placed in all compression members to safeguard them against the effects of small accidental bending moments that might crack and even fail an unreinforced member.

For most effective reinforcing action is essential that steel and concrete deform together, i.e., that there must be a sufficiently strong bond between the two materials to ensure that no relative movements of the steel bars and the surrounding concrete occur. This bond is provided by the relatively large chemical adhesion (黏结力) which develops at the steel concrete interface, by the natural roughness of the mill scale of hot-rolled reinforcing bars (热轧钢筋), and by the closely spaced rib-shaped surface deformations with which reinforcing bars are furnished in order to provide a high degree of interlocking (咬合) of the two materials.

Additional features which make for the satisfactory joint performance of steel and concrete are the following:

(1) The thermal expansion coefficients (线膨胀系数) of the two materials, about $6.5 \times 10^{-6}/K$ for steel vs. an average of $5.5 \times 10^{-6}/K$ for concrete, are sufficiently close to forestall cracking and other undesirable effects of differential thermal deformations.

(2) While the corrosion resistance of bare steel is poor, the concrete which surrounds the steel reinforcement provides excellent corrosion protection, minimizing corrosion (腐蚀) problems and corresponding (相应的) maintenance (维护) costs.

(3) The fire resistance of unprotected steel is impaired (受损) by its high thermal conductivity and by the fact that its strength decreases sizably at high temperatures. Conversely, the thermal conductivity of concrete is relatively low. Thus, damage caused by even prolonged fire exposure, if any, is generally limited to the outer layer of concrete, and a moderate amount of concrete cover provides sufficient thermal insulation (热绝缘) for the embedded reinforcement.

Steel is used in two different ways in concrete structures: as reinforcing steel and as prestressing steel. Reinforcing steel is placed in the forms prior to casting of the concrete. Stresses in the steel, as in the hardened concrete, are caused only by the loads on the structure, except for possible parasitic (附加) stresses from shrinkage (收缩) or similar causes. In contrast, in prestressed concrete structures large tension forces are applied to the reinforcement prior to letting it act jointly with the concrete in resisting external loads.

The most common type of reinforcing steel (as distinct from prestressing steel) is in the form of round bars, sometimes called rebars (螺纹钢筋), available in a large range of diameters (直径), from 10mm to 35mm for ordinary applications and in two heavy bar sizes of 44mm and 57mm. These bars are furnished (提供) with surface deformations for the purpose of increasing resistance to slip between steel and concrete. Minimum requirements for these deformations (spacing, projection, etc.) have been developed in experimental research. Different bar producers use different patterns, all of which satisfy these requirements.

Welding of rebars in making splices (拼接), or for convenience in fabricating (绑扎) reinforcing cages (钢筋笼) for placement in the forms, may result in metallurgical (化学) changes that reduce both strength and ductility, and special restrictions must be placed both on the type of steel used and the welding procedures. The provisions of ASTM A706 relate specifically to welding.

Reading material Ⅱ

The Red Square, the Central Square in Moscow

The Red Square is the central square in Moscow, Russia. The vast (广阔的) open space with distinguished (著名的) building complexes is grand. It joins the Kremlin (克里姆林宫) Wall on one side, and in front of it stands the granite (花岗岩) tomb (墓) of Lenin (列宁), where his embalmed body can be seen. On another side of the square is the Historical Museum (历史博物馆), and on the fourth, St. Basil's Cathedral (圣巴西尔大教堂).

The Red Square was built by Ivan Ⅲ at the end of the 15th century. The Czar (沙皇) sent for Italian architects and built the present wall of the Kremlin and two of the cathedrals. Then the building complex on the square was shaped and the layout of the Red Square was established.

The Red Square is world-famous, as the most important public events take place there. The anniversary of the Russian Revolution is celebrated there on Nov. 7th, and Labor Day on May 1st and 2nd. Colorful parades (游行), such as the one honoring the Soviet (苏联) astronauts (宇航员), are also held in the square.

The Red Square was not named by communists (共产党人), although red is their symbolic color. The name is an old one. In Russian the word for "red" is also used to mean "beautiful". So the square was known as "Beautiful Square". From this you can see the position of the square in the hearts of the Russian people.

Lesson 4 Building Components

Text

Materials and structural forms are combined to make up the various parts of a building, including the soil and foundations, load-carrying frame, skin, partitions, floors, and stairs, such as those shown in Fig 4.1. The building also has mechanical and electrical systems, such as elevators, heating and cooling systems, and lighting systems. The superstructure is the part of a building above ground; and the substructure and foundations are the parts of a building below ground.

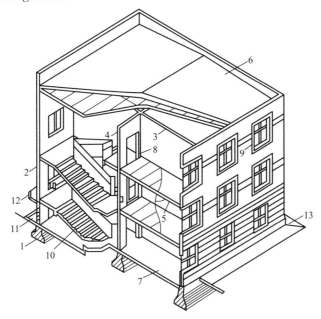

Fig 4.1 Components of a Building

1—foundation; 2—external wall; 3, 4—internal wall; 5—floor; 6—roof; 7—ground floor; 8—door; 9—window; 10—stair; 11—step; 12—canopy; 13—scatter water

Soils and foundations All buildings are supported on the ground, and therefore the nature of the soil becomes an extremely important consideration in the design of any building. The design of a foundation depends on many soil factors, such as the type of soil, soil stratification, thickness of soil layers and their compaction, and groundwater conditions.

Due to both the compaction and flow effects, buildings tend to settle. Uniform settlements are not so serious, but uneven settlements can have damaging effects—

the building may lean, walls and partitions may crack, windows and doors may become inoperative, and in the extreme, a building may collapse.

The great variability of soils has led to a variety of solutions to the foundations' problem. When the firm soil exists close to the surface, the simplest solution is to rest columns on a small slab of concrete [Fig 4.2(a)、(c)]. When the soil is softer, it is necessary to spread the column load over a greater area; in this case, a continuous-slab of concrete [Fig 4.2(b)、(d)] under the whole building is used. In cases when the soil near the surface is unable to support the weight of the building, piles of wood, steel, or concrete are driven down to firm soil [Fig 4.2(e)].

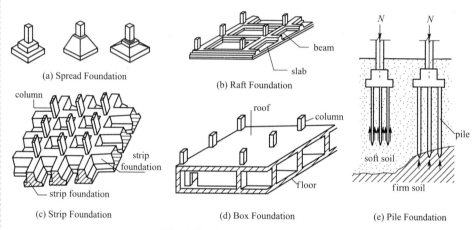

Fig 4.2　Types of Foundations

Load-carrying frame　Until the late 19th century, the exterior walls of a building were used as bearing walls to support the floors. This construction is still used in frame construction for houses. Bearing-wall construction limited the height of buildings because of the enormous wall thickness required[1]. Skeleton construction, consisting of steel beams and columns, was first used in 1889. As a consequence of skeleton construction, the enclosing walls become a "curtain wall" rather than a supporting function. Masonry was the curtain wall material until the 1930's, when light metal and glass curtain walls were used. After the introduction of the steel skeleton, the height of buildings continued to increase rapidly.

All tall buildings were built with the skeleton of steel until World War II. After the war, the shortage of steel and the improved quality of concrete led to tall buildings being built of reinforced concrete.

A change in attitude about skyscraper construction has brought a return to the use of the bearing wall. This perimeter wall, in fact, constitutes a bearing wall. One reason for this trend is that stiffness against the action of wind can be economically obtained by using the walls of the building as a tube[2].

Skin   The skin of a building consists of both transparent elements (windows) and opaque elements (walls) (Fig 4.3). The wall elements, which are used to cover the structure and are supported by it, are built of variety of materials: bricks, precast concrete, stones, opaque glass, plastics, steel, aluminum and so on.

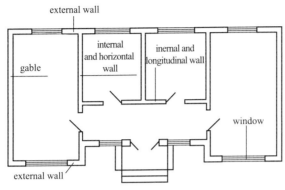

Fig 4.3   The Skin of a Building

Floors   The construction of the floors in a building depends on the basic structural frame that is used (Fig 4.4). In steel skeleton construction, floors are either slabs of concrete resting on steel beams or a deck consisting of corrugated steel with a concrete topping. In concrete construction, the floors are either slabs of concrete resting on concrete beams or a series of closely spaced concrete beams (ribs) in two directions topped with a thin concrete slab.

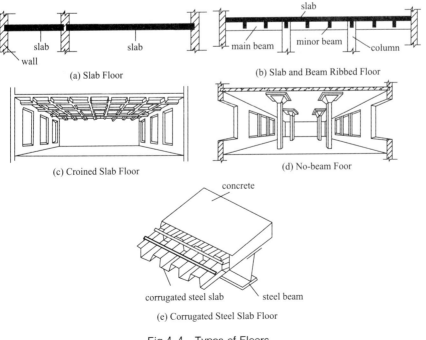

Fig 4.4   Types of Floors

Stairs Components of a staircase are shown in Fig 4.5. Stair is the vertical transport facilities which contact the two interfacing floors in the building. Stair should satisfy the vertical transportation in daily life and safely evacuate in emergency. Even with the elevator, high-rise buildings also need to set up the stairs. According to its forms, there are straight-running stairs, multi-running stairs, scissors-type stairs, spiral stairs etc (Fig 4.6). According to their different materials, there are: reinforced concrete stairs, steel stairs and wood stairs. Reinforced concrete stairs are frequently encountered in buildings because of more advantages than others in structural stiffness, refractory, cost, construction, forming etc.[3].

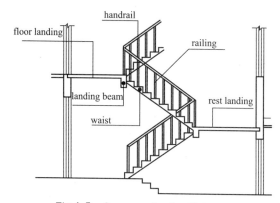

Fig 4.5 Components of a Staircase

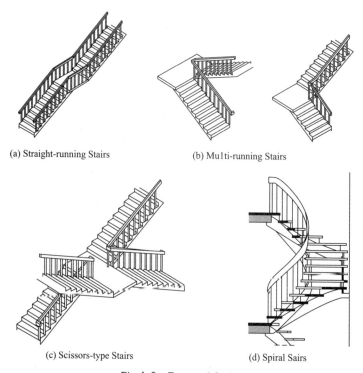

(a) Straight-running Stairs (b) Multi-running Stairs

(c) Scissors-type Stairs (d) Spiral Sairs

Fig 4.6 Forms of Stairs

New Words and Phrases

1. partition [pɑːˈtɪʃn] 分开，分割，隔墙，隔板
2. framework [ˈfreɪmwɜːk] 构架，框架，结构
3. superstructure [ˈsuːpəstrʌktʃə(r)] 上部结构
4. stratification [ˌstrætɪfɪˈkeɪʃn] 层理；成层
5. compaction [kəmˈpækʃn] 压实
6. composition [ˌkɒmpəˈzɪʃn] 组成
7. silt [sɪlt] 粉土
8. clay [kleɪ] 黏土
9. collapse [kəˈlæps] 倒塌
10. spread foundation [spred faʊnˈdeɪʃn] 扩展基础
11. raft foundation [rɑːft faʊnˈdeɪʃn] 筏板基础
12. pile [paɪl] 桩
13. exterior [ɪkˈstɪərɪə(r)] 外部的，外面的，外部，表面
14. bearing wall [ˈbeərɪŋ wɔːl] 承重墙
15. skeleton [ˈskelɪtn] 骨架
16. curtain wall [ˈkɜːtn wɔːl] 悬墙，幕墙
17. reinforced concrete [ˌriːɪnˈfɔːst ˈkɒŋkriːt] 钢筋混凝土
18. perimeter wall [pəˈrɪmɪtə wɔːl] 围墙
19. stability [stəˈbɪləti] 稳定性
20. opaque [əʊˈpeɪk] 不透明的，不透光的，不透明体
21. aluminum [əˈljuːmɪnəm] 铝
22. deck [dek] 甲板，舱面，桥面，层面
23. corrugate [ˈkɒrʊgeɪt] 弄皱，使起皱纹，起皱的，起波纹的
24. slab [slæb] 板
25. duct [dʌkt] 管道，通道，预应力筋孔
26. encounter [ɪnˈkaʊntə(r)] 遇到，碰到
27. refractory [rɪˈfræktəri] 耐火
28. canopy [ˈkænəpi] 雨篷
29. apron [ˈeɪprən] 窗台

Notes

[1] Bearing-wall construction limited the height of buildings because of

the enormous wall thickness required.

因为所需墙体的厚度很大,所以承重墙的结构限制了建筑物的高度。

[2] One reason for this trend is that stiffness against the action of wind can be economically obtained by using the walls of the building as a tube.

造成这种趋势的一个原因在于:当使用建筑物的墙体构成一个筒的时候,建筑物的抗风刚度可以非常经济地获得。

[3] Reinforced concrete stairs are frequently encountered in buildings because of more advantages than others in structural stiffness, refractory, cost, construction, forming etc.

钢筋混凝土楼梯在结构刚度、耐火、造价、施工、造型等方面具有较多的优点,应用最为普遍。

参 考 译 文

第4课 建筑构造

结合材料和结构形式组成一栋建筑物的不同部分,包括地基与基础、承重框架、围护构件、隔墙、楼地面和楼梯等,如图4.1所示。建筑物内部还有电气系统,例如电梯、供热与制冷系统和照明系统。上部结构是建筑物在地面以上的那个部分,下部结构和基础是建筑物在地面以下的部分。

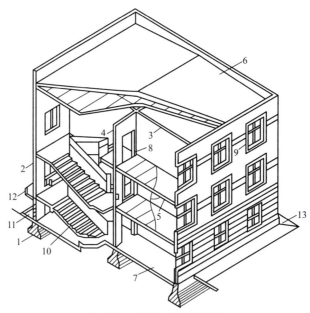

图 4.1 建筑物的组成部分

1—基础;2—外墙;3,4—内横墙;5—楼地面;6—屋顶;7—地坪;
8—门;9—窗;10—楼梯;11—台阶;12—雨篷;13—散水

地基与基础　所有建筑物都被支撑在地面上，因此土壤的性质在建筑物的设计中成为一个非常重要的考虑因素。基础的设计取决于地基土的很多因素，如地基土的类型、层理、各土层的厚度及其压缩性，以及地下水的条件等。

由于压实和滑移作用的影响，建筑物往往要产生沉降。均匀沉降不会产生很严重的后果，但是不均匀沉降有破坏性影响——建筑物可能倾斜，外墙和隔墙可能开裂，门窗可能被破坏，在极端的情况下，建筑物可能会倒塌。

由于不同建筑物下的土质不同，因而解决基础问题的办法也是各种各样的。当坚硬的土接近地表时，最简单的解决办法是直接在一个很小的混凝土板上设置柱子[图 4.3(a)、(c)]。当土比较软的时候，就需要基底面积较大的基础来承担荷载，在这种情况下，可以在整个建筑物下设置连续混凝土板[图 4.2(b)、(d)]。当接近地表的土层无法支撑建筑物重量的时，将使用打到坚硬土层里的深基础，如木桩、钢桩或混凝土桩[图 4.2(e)]。

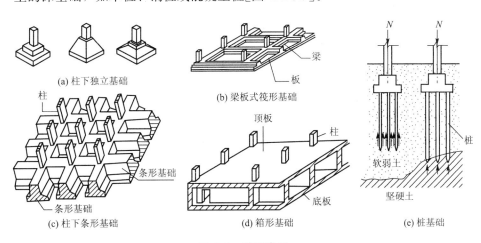

图 4.2　基础类型

承重框架　直到 19 世纪后期，建筑物的外墙仍被用作支撑楼面的承重墙。这种建筑形式现在仍然作为住宅建筑的框架结构。因为所需墙厚很大，所以承重墙的结构限制了建筑物的高度。由钢梁和钢柱组成的钢骨架结构，在 1889 年第一次被使用。钢骨架结构的使用，使得原来的承重墙变成了"幕墙"，而不再起承重作用。到 20 世纪 30 年代轻金属和玻璃幕墙开始使用之前，砌体一直作为幕墙材料使用。引进钢骨架后，建筑物的高度继续迅猛增加。

直到第二次世界大战，所有的高楼大厦均使用钢骨架。战争结束后，由于钢材的短缺和混凝土质量的日益提高，使高层建筑开始使用钢筋混凝土来建造。

摩天大楼的骨架形式的一个转变，使得建筑又重新回到使用承重墙上来。实际上，这种围墙构成了承重墙。造成这种趋势的一个原因在于：当建筑物的墙体构成一个筒的时候，可以非常经济地获得抗风刚度。

围护结构　建筑物的围护结构是由透明的部分(窗)和不透明的部分(墙)组成的(图 4.3)。用来围护结构并由结构来支撑的墙，可以由各种材料来建造：砖、混凝土预制构件、石材、不透明玻璃、塑料、钢、铝等。

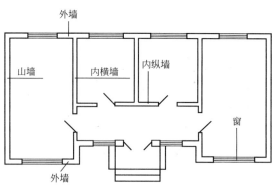

图 4.3　围护结构

楼板　建筑物中楼板层的结构形式取决于所采用的承重框架结构（图 4.4）。在钢结构中，楼板要么是置于钢梁上的混凝土板，要么是压型钢板混凝土组合楼板。在混凝土结构中，楼板是梁板式楼板或是置于井字梁上的混凝土薄板。

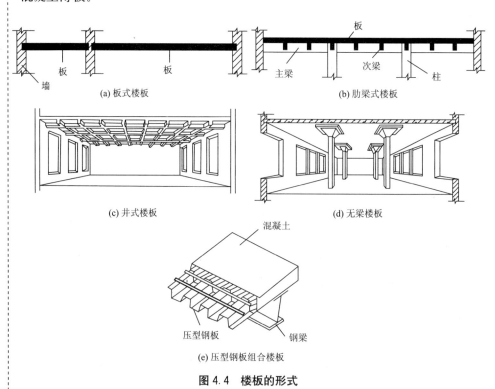

图 4.4　楼板的形式

楼梯　楼梯的组成如图 4.5 所示。楼梯是建筑物联系上下层的垂直交通设施。楼梯应满足人们日常生活时的垂直交通和紧急时的安全疏散要求。在设电梯的高层建筑中也必须同样设置楼梯。楼梯根据其平面形式可分成：单跑直楼梯、多跑楼梯、剪刀式楼梯、螺旋楼梯等（图 4.6）；根据其材料不同可分为钢筋混凝土楼梯、钢楼梯和木楼梯等,其中钢筋混凝土楼梯在结构刚度、耐火、造价、施工、造型等方面具有较多的优点,应用最为普遍。

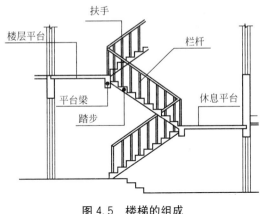

图 4.5 楼梯的组成

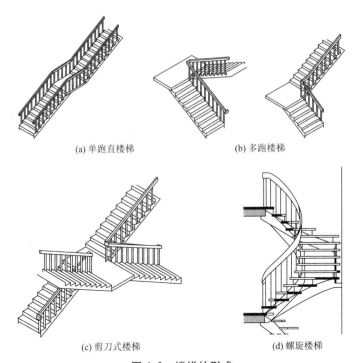

图 4.6 楼梯的形式

Reading material Ⅰ

Different Kinds of Homes

Home is a word that can mean many different things. Home can be a tree, a cave, a boat, a hole in the ground, a house in the country, or an apartment in a tall building.

Homes can be made of many things—branches, leaves, dirt, stones, wood, bricks, or steel and glass. Our homes protect us from the weather and from our enemies.

People who live in different kinds of places need different kinds of homes. In hot countries, people need houses that are cool. In cold countries, people need warm houses.

People have always built their homes with the materials that were easily available. Prehistoric people who lived in or near forests used trees and branches. In rocky places, people built their shelters with stones and rocks, or they used caves that already existed.

Some prehistoric people lived in hot and flat places. They needed to protect themselves from the hot sun and from wild animals. At first, they lived in or under trees. Later, they learned to dig holes that were big enough to live in. Then they covered the holes with branches and leaves.

People who lived in the mountains were usually able to find large caves. They covered the entrance (入口) to the cave with animal skins, which kept out the rain and the snow and the wind. Caves were warm in the winter and cool in the summer.

When cave people moved to new places, they left tools and other things in their old caves. Archeologists (考古学家) have found the bones and teeth of people and animals in caves. They have also found pictures on cave-walls that tell about the people and the animals that existed in prehistoric times.

Of course, caves didn't have all the wonderful things that are available in our modern world. Cave people didn't have refrigerators or soft beds or bathtubs (澡盆). But they could keep their food cool in the ice and snow, and they could make comfortable beds with leafy (多叶的) branches and furry (毛皮的) blankets (绒被). And they did not need bathtubs because many caves had rivers in them.

Although holes in the ground and mountain caves weren't the most wonderful homes that have ever existed, the people who lived in them were probably very happy. And that's the most important thing about "home". It doesn't have to be huge and beautiful. It can be in the city or the country. "Home" is a place that means peace and comfort and love to the people who live there.

Reading material II

The Taj Mahal, One of the Most Beautiful Buildings in the World

Almost everyone has read about the Taj Mahal (泰姬陵) in India. It is one of the most beautiful buildings in the world. Over three hundred years ago, Shah Jehan (沙·贾汗) built the Taj Mahal as the tomb for his wife.

Shah Jehan wanted his wife's tomb perfect. He did not care about time or money. He brought together workmen from all Asia. Altogether, over 20,000 men worked on the buildings, and it took them twenty-two years to finish it.

The building rests on a platform of red sandstone. Four thin white towers rise from the corner of the platform. A large dome (穹顶) rests from the centre of the building. Around this large dome there are four smaller ones.

The building is made of fine white and colored marble (大理石). It has eight sides and many arches. There is an open corridor just inside the outer walls. From this corridor, the visitor looks through the marble screen to a central room. The bodies of Shah Jehan and his wife lie in a tomb below this room.

A beautiful garden surrounds the Taj Mahal. The green trees make the marble look even whiter. In front of the main entrance to the building there is a long, narrow pool. If you look in this pool, you can see all the beauty of the Taj Mahal in the reflection (倒影) from the water.

Many people think the Taj Mahal is most beautiful at sunset. Then the marble picks up the color of the sunset, and the building and its reflection in the pool gleam like red jewels.

Lesson 5　Building Engineering Surveying

Text

Surveying is one of the oldest activities of the civil engineering and remains a primary component of civil engineering.

Before any civil engineering project can be designed, a survey of the site must be made. Some engineering projects, for example, highways, dams, or tunnels, may require extensive surveying in order to determine the best location and the most economical route.

There are two kinds of surveying: plane and geodetic. The most primary area perhaps is plane surveying. In plane surveying, we consider the fundamentals of measuring distance, angle, direction, and elevation. These measured quantities are then used to determine position, slope, area, and volume—the basic parameters of civil engineering design and construction. Plane surveying is the measurement of the earth's surface as though it were a flat surface without a curvature. Within areas of about 20 kilometers square—meaning a square, each side of which is 20 kilometers long—the effects of the earth's curvature are negligible relative to the positional accuracy[1]. For larger areas, however, a geodetic survey which takes into account the curvature of the earth must be made (Fig 5.1).

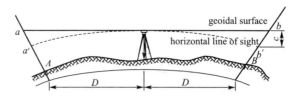

Fig 5.1　The Sketch Map of the Effects of the Earth's Curvature on Geodetic Survey

The different kinds of measurements in a survey include distances, elevations (heights of features within the area), boundaries (both man-made and natural), and other physical characteristics of the site.

In plane surveying, the principal measuring device for distance is the steel tape (Fig 5.2). The men who hold the steel tape during a survey are still usually called chainmen. They generally level the tape by means of plumb bobs, which are lead weights attached to a line that give the direction of gravity. When especially accurate results are required, other means of support, such as a tripod—a stand with three legs (Fig 5.3) can be used.

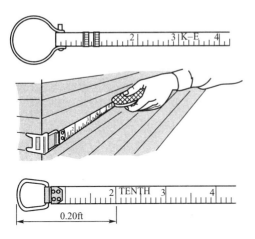

Fig 5.2 Styles of End Fasteners on Steel Tapes

Fig 5.3 The Sketch Map of Tripod

The indicated length of a steel tape is in fact exactly accurate only at a temperature of 20 centigrade, so temperature readings are often taken during a survey to correct the distances by allowing for expansion or contraction of the tape.

Distances between elevations are measured in a horizontal plane. In the diagram alongside, the distance between the two hills is measured from points A to B rather than from points A to C to D to B (Fig 5.4).

Fig 5.4 The Distance Between the Two Hills

Angles are measured in degrees of arc. Two different systems are in use. One is the sexagesimal system that employs 360°, each degree consisting of 60 minutes and each minute of 60 seconds. The other is the centesimal system that employs 400°, each degree consisting of 100 minutes and each minute of 100 seconds. A special telescopic instrument that gives more accurate readings of angles than the transit is called a theodolite (Fig 5.5).

In addition to cross hairs, transits and theodolites have markings called stadia hairs (Fig 5.6). The stadia hairs are parallel to the horizontal cross hairs. The transitman sights a rod. The stadia hairs are fixed to represent a distance that is usually a hundred times each of the marks on the rod. That is, when the stadia hairs are in line with a mark on the rod that reads 2.5, the transit is 250 meters from the rod. Stadia surveys are particularly useful in determining contour lines, which on a map enclose areas of equal elevation.

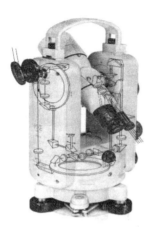

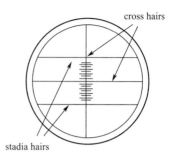

Fig 5.5　A Theodolite　　　Fig 5.6　Markings of Transits and Theodolites

Contour maps can be made in the field by means of a plane-table alidade. The alidade is a telescope with a vertical circle and stadia hairs. It is mounted on a straightedged metal plate that can be kept parallel to the line of sight. The surveyor can mark his readings of distances and elevations on a plane (or flat) table that serves as a drawing board. When the marks representing equal elevations are connected, the surveyor has made a contour map.

Heights or elevations are determined by means of a surveyor's level, another kind of telescope with a bubble leveling device parallel to the telescope. A bubble level, which is similar to a carpenter's level, is a tube containing fluid that has an air bubble in it. When the bubble is centered in the middle of the tube, the device is level. The surveyor sights a rule called a level rod through the telescope. The rod is marked off to show units of measure in large, clear numbers. The spaces between the marks usually are alternately black and white in order to increase visibility. The number that the surveyor reads on the level rod, less the height of his or her instrument, is the vertical elevation[2] (Fig 5.7).

Modern technology has been used for surveying instruments that measure distance by means of light or sound waves. Aerial photography is another modern method of surveying.

Geodetic surveying is much more complex than plane surveying. It involves measuring a network of triangles that are based on points on the earth's surface. The triangulation is then reconciled by mathematical calculations with the shape of the earth. This shape, incidentally, is not a perfect sphere but an imaginary surface, slightly flattened at the poles, that represents mean sea level as though it were continued even under the continental land masses.

In addition to measuring surfaces for civil engineering projects, it is often

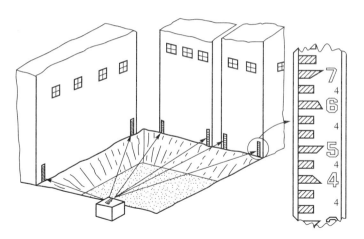

Fig 5.7 Level Setup to Maintain a Watch Over Building Settlements During Excavation

necessary to make a geological survey. This involves determining the composition of the soil and rock that underlie the surface at the construction site. The nature of the soil, the depth of which bedrock is located, and the existence of faults or underground streams are subsurface factors that help civil engineers determine the type and size of the structural foundations or the weight of the structure that can rest on them.

With the development of science and technology, more advanced surveying equipments appeared. GPS (Global Positioning System) navigator is one of them. It combines the global positioning technology with computer, space and modern communication technologies. Global Positioning System consists of GPS Satellites, Ground Station, and GPS User (Fig 5.8).

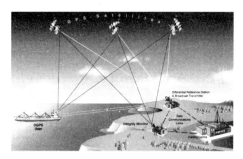

Fig 5.8 Global Positioning System (GPS Satellites, Ground Station, GPS User)

New Words and Phrases

1. accuracy   [ˈækjərəsi]   准确，精确；准确度，精度
2. geodetic   [ˌdʒiːəˈdetɪk]   测地学的，测量的
3. feature   [ˈfiːtʃə(r)]   地势，地形
4. characteristic   [ˌkærəktəˈrɪstɪk]   特有的，表示特性的
                                              特点，特征，特性

5. acre	[ˈeɪkə(r)]	英亩（合4,047平方米，6.07亩）
6. plumb	[plʌm]	铅锤，铅弹，垂直的，使垂直，探测，垂直
7. tripod	[ˈtraɪpɒd]	三脚桌，三角架
8. sexagesima	[ˌseksəˈdʒesɪmə]	六十的，六十进位的，以六十为分母的分数
9. theodolite	[θɪˈɒdəlaɪt]	[测] 精密经纬仪
10. stadia	[ˈsteɪdɪə]	视距，视距仪器，stadium的复数
11. interval	[ˈɪntəvl]	（空间的）间隔，距离，时间间隔
12. straightedg	[ˈstreɪtedʒ]	直尺，标尺
13. less	[les]	减去，扣除；不计
less the height of his or her instrument		可译成"减去仪器高"

Notes

[1] Plane surveying is the measurement of the earth's surface as though it were a flat surface without a curvature. Within areas of about 20 kilometers square—meaning a square, each side of which is 20 kilometers long—the effects of the earth's curvature are negligible relative to the positional accuracy.

平面测量是把地球表面当作一个没有曲率的平面进行测量的。在一个边长为20km的正方形区域中，地球曲率对位置精确度的影响可以忽略不计。

[2] The number that the surveyor reads on the level rod, less the height of his or her instrument, is the vertical elevation.

测量员从水准尺上所得的读数，减去仪器高，即为垂直高程。

参考译文

第5课　建筑工程测量

测量是土木工程中最古老的领域之一，也是土木工程的一个重要组成部分。

在设计任何土木工程项目之前，必须先对建筑场地进行测量。有些工程项目，例如公路、水坝或隧道，可能需要广泛地测量，以便确定最佳的地点和最经济的路线。

常用的测量方法有两种：平面测量和大地测量。其中最主要的方法是平面测量。在平面测量中，最基本的工作是距离测量、角度测量、方向测量和高程测量。这些测量结果被用来确定位置、坡度、面积和体积这些土木工程设计和施工的基本参数。平面测量是把地球表面当作一个没有曲率的平面进行测量的。在一个边长为20km的正方形区域中，地球曲率对位置精确度的影响可以忽略不计。然而在比较大的区域中,则应该采用考虑地球曲率影响的大地测量(图5.1)。

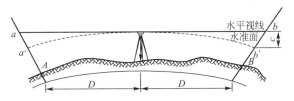

图5.1 地球曲率对大地测量影响示意图

在测量中,测定内容包括距离、高程(测量范围内各地形的高度)、边界(人造的和自然的)和现场上的其他物理特征。

在平面测量中,主要的测距工具是钢卷尺(图5.2)。在测量工作中用钢尺的人还常被称为测量员。一般是用垂球来调平钢尺。垂球是上端系有一根指示重力方向铅制重物的细绳。当需要特别精确的结果时,可以使用其他仪器,例如三脚架(图5.3)。

实际上钢尺的标称长度只有在20℃时才是准确的,所以在测量时常常要记下实际温度,以便酌量加减钢尺的膨胀或收缩率来校正距离读数。

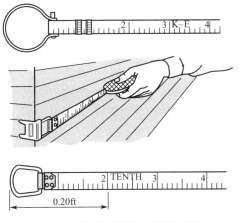

图5.2 钢卷尺不同端部示意图

图5.3 三脚架示意图

高程之间的距离用水平测量法来测量。如图5.4所示,两座小山之间的距离是测量从 A 点到 B 点的距离,而不是从 A 点到 C 点到 D 点再到 B 点的距离。

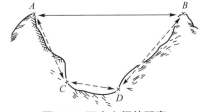

图5.4 两山之间的距离

角度用弧度来度量。当前使用的有两种分度制:一种是60分度制,共360度,每度有60分,每分有60秒;另一种是100分度制,共400度,每度有100分,每分有100秒。此外还有一种比经纬仪更加准确的仪器,这种仪器称为精密经纬仪(图5.5)。

经纬仪和精密经纬仪除了有十字丝外,还有叫做视距丝的刻度(图5.6)。

视距丝与十字丝的水平丝平行。测量员需要照准水准尺。视距丝是固定的，通常用于指出相当于水准尺上一个刻度的一百倍的距离。这就是说，当视距丝与水准尺上的标记2.5重合时，则经纬仪与水准尺相距250米。视距测量在确定等高线方面特别有用。等高线是指在图上把高程相同的区域围封起来的线。

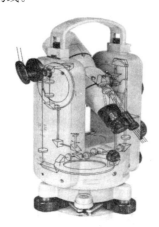

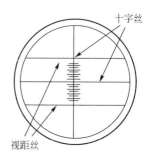

图5.5　精密经纬仪　　　　图5.6　经纬仪和精密经纬仪的刻度示意图

等高线图可以用大平板（照准）仪在现场绘制。照准仪是一种装有一个垂直圆环和视距丝的望远镜。它安装在一块与视线保持平行的直边金属板上。测量员可在一块用作绘图板的平板上记下距离和高程的读数。当把高程相等的标记连在一起时，等高线图就绘制好了。

高度，即高程，是测量员用水准仪来测定的。这种水准仪其实是另外一种望远镜，它装有一个与望远镜平行的气泡水准仪。气泡水准仪与木工的水平尺相似，它是一个装有液体且液体里面有一个气泡的管子。当气泡在管内居中时，仪器就是水平的。测量员通过望远镜瞄准一个叫做水准尺的标杆。该标杆上已用大而清楚的数字标出度量单位。为了提高明视度，标记之间的空隙通常交替地涂以黑白两种颜色。测量员从水准尺上所得的读数，减去仪器高，即为垂直高程（图5.7）。

现代技术已被用于测量仪器，它们借助光或声波来测量距离。航空摄影术是另一种现代测量方法。

大地测量要比平面测量复杂得多。它包括根据地球表面各点而测量出的三角网，然后通过数学计算使三角测量符合地球形状。顺便讲一下，地球形状并不是一个准确的球形，而是一个假想的、两极略扁的表面，它代表平均海平面，因此假设它是连续的，甚至伸展到大片陆地下面。

土木工程项目除了需要进行地表测量外，还常常需要进行地质勘测。地质勘测包括确定施工现场地表下面的土壤和岩石的成分。土壤的性质、基岩的深度以及有无断层或地下河流，都是一些地下因素，这些因素可帮助土木工程师确定构筑物基础的类型、大小或其所能承受的构筑物的重量。

随着科学技术的发展，更先进的测量仪器出现了。GPS（全球卫星导航

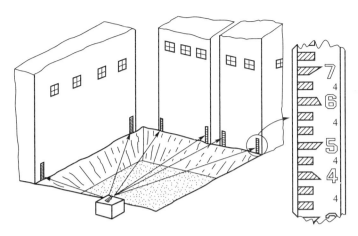

图 5.7 水准仪基坑开挖期间建筑物沉降观测示意图

定位系统）就是其中之一。它包含计算机的全球定位技术、空间和现代沟通技术。卫星导航系统由导航卫星、地面站、用户设备组成（图 5.8）。

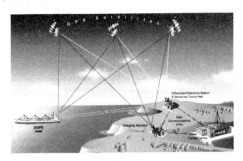

图 5.8

Reading material I

The Great Wall

The Great Wall of China is the biggest structure that man has ever built. It is 15 feet thick and as tall as a house. It stretches for about 1500 miles across the mountains and valleys of northern China. Every 200 or 300 yards there is a tall watchtower（瞭望塔）. The entire wall is made of earth, stones and bricks. Different parts of the wall were built at different times, but all of them were built many hundreds of years ago-before there were not machines to help with the building. Thousands of men worked with their hands to build this long wall.

Why did they build it?

The wall was built by order of the Chinese emperors to keep out the enemies in the north, who had been riding their horses into China, killing people and stealing things. After the Great Wall was built, the people of

China felt safer. If an enemy approached the wall, smoke signals would be passed from watchtower to watchtower. A signal fire would be lighted if an attack came at night. An alarm would be sounded, and the emperor's army would rush to defend the wall.

Time went on, and for a while China has become one of the richest, biggest, and most beautiful countries in the world.

In China at that time people lived in great and clean cities. Garbage was carried away. It did not pile up in the streets. Parks were kept green and seat. Water was used to keep the dust down and to wash the streets clean. Some of the rulers (统治者) lived in beautiful palaces with gold roofs. The rest of the world, or much of it, lived in dirty huts (小屋) on dirty streets.

The Chinese invented compass, gunpowder (火药), paper and printing. They discovered the value of vaccinations (接种疫苗). They had public baths and clocks. And they had their Great Wall to protect themselves and their possessions (财产), the wall that was supposed to keep the enemies from riding in and destroying things.

Unfortunately, the Great Wall didn't always protect the Chinese people. It stretched so far and through such lonely places that enemies sometimes broke through. Finally, the Chinese stopped depending on their wall.

Walls sometimes keep out good things, as well as bad things. In the years that had passed since the building of the Great Wall, the people outside China had discovered some things that the Chinese did not know. The Chinese realized that they had remained (保持) separate from the rest of the world long enough. They began to exchange ideas with the rest of the world. It was good for everybody that they did. The Chinese learned about machines. The rest of the world brought back ideas from China that led to fire departments, modern street cleaning, the printing press, and new medicines.

Reading material II

The Palace Museum, Ancient and Magnificent Buildings

Beijing's Forbidden City, now known as the Palace Museum, has a history of more than five hundred and eighty years. It is said that the rulers of the Yuan Dynasty were the first to have their palace built here. Begun in 1407, a new set of palace was built in 1420 when Emperor Yong Le of the Ming Dynasty decided to move his capital from Nanjing to Beijing.

All of the timber (木材) needed for the huge columns and beams of the palace buildings were shipped from the forests in Yunnan and Sichuan Provinces. This gigantic (巨大的) project took as long as thirteen years to finish, employing as many as two hundred thousand workmen. In the subsequent years, repairs and improvements on the palace halls were made by the succeeding emperors. The imperial palace grounds, or the Forbidden City as it is sometimes called, occupy an area of seven hundred and twenty thousand square meters with a total of nine thousand halls and rooms built on them.

Standing in the centre of Beijing, these magnificent (宏伟的) buildings are manifestations (表现) of the wisdom and creativity of the labouring people.

Lesson 6 Building Structures

Text

A structure is the part of a building that carries its weight. We should remember that anything built is a structure. A structure may be a dwelling house, or a pyramid in Egypt, or a dam on a river. A building is a structure with a roof and much of civil engineering structural design is the design of building structure. The part of the building that holds up the weight and load is called the structural part. Parts such as windows that do not hold up the building are the non-structural parts.

Building structures are classified into many forms according to the different materials, such as concrete structure, steel structure and masonry structure. Concrete structure is aslo classified into three forms, such as reinforced concrete, prestressed concrete and plain concrete.

1. Reinforced Concrete Structures

In reinforced concrete structures, steel reinforcing bars are embedded in concrete structures where tensile stress may occur to make the good compressive strength of concrete structures fully put into action[1].

Generally speaking, reinforced concrete structures possess the following features: large dead mass, high stiffness, good durability, long curing period, easily cracked and so on.

Reinforced concrete systems are composed of a variety of concrete structural elements that, when synthesized, produce a total system. The components can be broadly classified: floor slabs, beams, columns, walls and foundations shown in Fig 6.1.

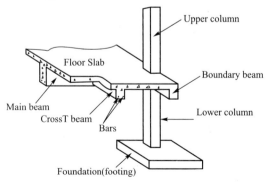

Fig 6.1 Typical Reinforced Concrete Framing Structure

Because of the ways that buildings are made to hold up weight, building structures can divide into different types, such as framed structure, shear wall structure, wall-framed structure and tube structure[2].

Frame structure　Structural systems composed of elements that are long compared with their cross-sectional dimensions are referred to as frame structure, such as beam and column. The elements of a fram structure are defined as linear element since they can transfer the support of loads in only one direction, that is, along the length of the element shown in Fig 6.2.

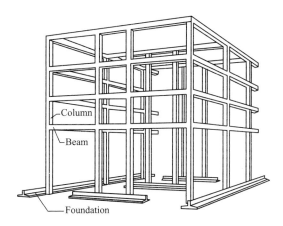

Fig 6.2　Frame Structure

Shear wall structure　Concrete continuous vertical walls may serve both architecturally as partitions and structurally to carry gravity and lateral loading. Their very high inplane stiffness and strength make them ideally suited for bracing multistory buildings and tall buildings. In a shear wall structure, such walls are entirely responsible for the lateral load resistance of the buildings. They act as vertical cantilevers in the form of separate planar walls, and as nonplanar assemblies of connected walls around elevator, stair, and service shafts. Because they are much stiffer horizontally than rigid frames, shear wall structure can be economical up to 35 stories shown in Fig 6.3.

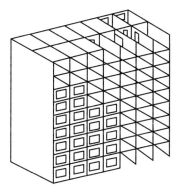

Fig 6.3　Shear Wall Structure

Wall-frame structure When shear walls are combined with frames, the walls, which tend to deflect in a flexural configuration, and the frame, which tend to deflect in a shear mode, are constrained to adopt a common deflected shape by the horizontal rigidity of the girder and slabs. As a consequence, the walls and frames interact horizontally, especially at the top, to produce a stiffer and stronger structure. The interacting wall-frame combination is appropriate for buildings in the 40 to 60 story range, well beyond that of rigid frames or shear walls alone shown in Fig 6.4.

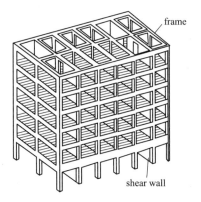

Fig 6.4　Wall-frame Structure

Tube structure The maximum efficiency of the total structure of a tall building, for both strength and stiffness to resist wind load can be achieved only if all column element can be connected to each other in such a way that the entire building acts as a hollow tube or rigid box in projecting out of the ground, that is the tube structure shown in Fig 6.5.

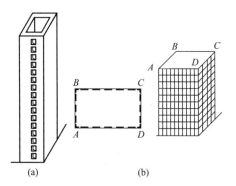

Fig 6.5　Tube Structure

Prestressed concrete Prestressed concrete is basically concrete in which internal stresses of a suitable magnitude and distribution are introduction so that the stresses resulting from external loads are counteracted to a desired degree. In reinforced concrete members, the prestress is commonly introduced by tensioning the steel reinforcement. Method of prestressing the concrete:

the pre-tension method and the post-tension method.

The use of high strength material results in a reduction in the cross sectional dimensions of prestressed concrete structural elements, with reduced dead weight of the material, longer spans become technically and economically practicable.

2. Masonry Structure

The earliest use of masonry can be traced back to two thousand years ago in China. Before the use of reinforced concrete, masonry such as stones, bricks were the main construction materials as well as wood. Even in the modern time, due to its good quality of heat preservation and easy manufacture and construction, most countries especially the developing countries are using it as main material for civil buildings.

The masonry structure takes the role place in the developing countries for its lower cost. But as known to all, masonry materials such as brick or block is a type of brittle material. Its compressive capacity is strong, however, its tensile capacity is weak and its poor deformability or ductility characteristic. Buildings built by ductile materials can endure severe earthquake and would not fall down even seriously damaged, but those built by brittle materials would suddenly fall down once the earthquake load exceeds its resistant capacity. Thus, some strict limitations have to be specified to these areas where they may encounter severe earthquakes.

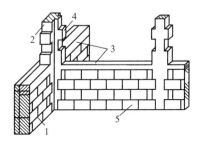

Fig 6.6 Composite Masonry (CM) Structure
1—longitudinal masonry wall; 2—constructional column;
3—ring beam; 4— joint motor; 5—horizontal masonry wall

Researches had advanced several approaches to get competent ductile masonry structures for earthquake region. One of them is composite masonry (CM) structure, shown in Fig 6.6. The CM structure is a structure that has some small reinforced concrete columns to be inserted into the masonry wall and to envelop the wall with beams.[3] The position, dimension, number, and reinforcement of the RC columns might to be decided by structural calculation. Unlike the masonry-infilled RC frame structure, the masonry in CM structure is constructed before concrete pouring. After the pouring of columns and beams, the masonry wall is well connected with the concrete members through the shear keys in columns and horizontal connecting steel bars lay between columns and block units in joint motor. By this way, both concrete and masonry members of the structure are restricted to each other and can deform harmoniously. Due to the property of restriction, we named the RC column as constructional column and the beam as ring beam. In such a structure, cracks are expected to take place firstly in masonry, then in RC columns after diagonal cracks penetrate the masonry and begin to slide. This approach is widely accepted and used in China. The trace investigations show that even the temperature cracks are hardly to be found in such buildings, which means excellent integrality of the structures.

The cheapest masonry building material is brick, and brick is the widest used material in China. So, in the early time of this CM research work, the main studies were focus on brick. But recently, in order to protect soil resource and ecological environment, Chinese government is urging their people to use energy-saving materials such as hollow concrete block instead of brick. The hollow concrete block is world wide used, but in China the utilizing is very limited and the total amount of production only account for less than 1 per cent of all wall materials. The use of hollow concrete block has at least four favorable benefits: ①saving soil land (one has estimated that the use of hollow concrete instead of brick can save more than 10 thousand hectares land); ②saving energy (hollow concrete block only consumes 46% energy of brick's. If half of bricks are to be replaced by hollow concrete block, 30 million Tons of raw coal can be saved in China); ③reducing 22%～40% weight of the building, thus decreasing earthquake forces in earthquake; ④shortening construction period and saving more than 10 percent of construction fund. These benefits show that the application future of hollow concrete block is very attractive.

3. Steel Structures

Steel structure refers to a broad of building structures in which steel plays the leading role. Steel offers much better compression and tension than concrete and enables lighter construction. Steel structures use three-dimensional trusses, so they can be larger than reinforced concrete counterparts.

New Words and Phases

1. compressive strength　　　　　[kəm'presiv streŋθ]　　　　抗压强度

2. tension [ˈtenʃn] 拉力，张力
3. reinforcement [ˌriːɪnˈfɔːsmənt] 钢筋，加强，加固
4. dead mass [ded mæs] 自重
5. horizontal [ˌhɒrɪˈzɒntl] 水平，横向
6. curing period [ˈkjʊərɪŋ ˈpɪəriəd] 养护期
7. transfer [trænsˈfɜː(r)] 传递
8. column [ˈkɒləm] 柱
9. masonry [ˈmeɪsənri] 砌体
10. floor slabs [flɔː(r) slæbz] 楼板
11. durability [ˌdjʊərəˈbɪləti] 耐久性
12. plain concrete [pleɪn kɒnkriːt] 素混凝土，无筋混凝土
13. prestressed concrete [pˈriːstrest ˈkɒnkriːt] 预应力混凝土
14. footing [ˈfʊtɪŋ] 基脚，底座
15. shear [ʃɪə(r)] 剪切，剪力
16. broadly [ˈbrɔːdli] 广泛的
17. synthesized [ˈsɪnθɪsaɪzd] 被组合
18. proportion [prəˈpɔːʃn] 比例
19. structural calculation [ˈstrʌktʃərəl ˌkælkjʊˈleɪʃən] 结构计算
20. exterior [ɪkˈstɪəriə(r)] 外部
21. aesthetically [esˈθetɪklɪ] 审美地
22. isolated footing [ˈaɪsəˌleɪtɪd ˈfʊtɪŋ] 独立基础
23. cantilever [ˈkæntɪliːvə(r)] 悬臂梁
24. planar wall [ˈpleɪnə(r) wɔːl] 平面墙
25. ductility [dʌkˈtɪlɪti] 延性
26. brace [breɪs] 支撑
27. joint motor [dʒɔɪnt ˈməʊtə(r)] 马牙槎
28. constructional column [kənˈstrʌkʃənəl ˈkɒləm] 构造柱
29. ring beam [rɪŋ biːm] 圈梁

Notes

[1] In reinforced concrete structures, steel reinforcing bars are embedded in concrete structures where tensile stress may occur to make the good compressive strength of concrete structures fully put into action.

在钢筋混凝土结构中，利用钢筋埋在混凝土结构中的可能产生拉应力的地方来使混凝土良好的抗压强度得以充分发挥。

[2] Because of the ways that buildings are made to hold up weight, building structures can divide into different types, such as framed structure,

shear wall structure, wall-framed structure and tube structure.

根据结构承受荷载方式的不同，建筑结构可以分为不同的类型，如框架结构、剪力墙结构、框架-剪力墙结构和筒体结构等。

[3] The CM structure is a structure that has some small reinforced concrete columns to be inserted into the masonry wall and to envelop the wall with beams.

复合砌体结构是在砌体墙中嵌入小型的钢筋混凝土柱，并使柱和梁连接成对围护墙体的结构形式。

参 考 译 文

第6课 建 筑 结 构

结构是建筑物的一部分，它支撑建筑物的重量。要记住的是任何建造出的东西都是一种结构。结构可能是一幢住宅、埃及的金字塔或者是河上的大坝。房屋是带有屋盖的结构。而许多土木工程结构设计就是房屋结构设计。建筑物中承受重量和荷载的部分称为结构部分。像窗户这样的非承重部分是非结构部分。

房屋结构按照不同的材料可以分为很多种形式，如混凝土结构、钢结构和砌体结构。混凝土结构可以分为3种类型，如钢筋混凝土结构、预应力混凝土结构和素混凝土结构。

1. 钢筋混凝土结构

在钢筋混凝土结构中，利用钢筋埋在混凝土结构中的可能产生拉应力的地方来使混凝土良好的抗压强度得以充分发挥。

一般来说，钢筋混凝土结构具有以下特点：自重大、刚度高、好的耐久性、较长的养护期、易开裂等。

钢筋混凝土结构是由大量混凝土构件组合而成的一个整体。这些构件大致可划分为楼板、梁、柱、墙、基础等，如图6.1所示。

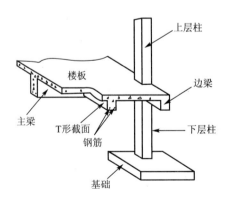

图6.1 钢筋混凝土框架结构

根据结构承受荷载方式的不同，建筑结构可以分为不同的类型，如框架结构、剪力墙结构、框架-剪力墙结构和筒体结构等[2]。

框架结构 由比其横截面尺寸长的构件组成的结构体系称为框架结构，如梁和柱。框架结构的构件被认为是直线构件，因为它们能仅在一个方向上即构件长度方向上传递荷载，如图 6.2 所示。

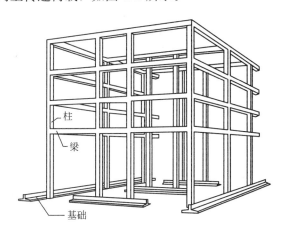

图 6.2 框架结构

剪力墙结构 混凝土竖向连续墙可以在建筑上起到分割的作用或者在结构上起到承受重力和侧向荷载的作用。由于具有非常高的平面内刚度和强度，它们非常适用于多层和高层建筑。在剪力墙结构中，剪力墙完全用来抵抗建筑物承受的侧向荷载。它们以独立平面墙体的形式像悬臂梁一样工作，并且作为非平面组合联系围绕电梯间、楼梯间和服务用竖井的墙。因为剪力墙的水平刚度比框架的高，所以剪力墙结构能非常经济地建造到 35 层，如图 6.3 所示。

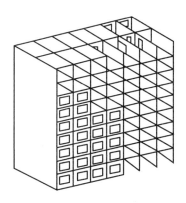

图 6.3 剪力墙结构

框架-剪力墙结构 当剪力墙结构与框架结合，剪力墙就趋于弯曲变形，而框架则趋于剪切变形，它们都被大梁和板的水平刚度所约束而表现出共同的挠曲形态。以此作为推理依据，剪力墙和框架水平向的相互作用，特别是在结构顶端，将产生出更高的刚度和强度。框架和剪力墙的组合适用于 40 层到 60 层的高层建筑结构，比单独的框架结构和剪力墙结构适用的层数要多，如图 6.4 所示。

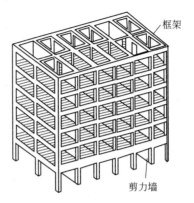

图 6.4　框架-剪力墙结构

筒体结构　高层建筑所有结构类型中用于抵抗风荷载的，要使强度和刚度能到达最高，只有将所有竖向构件相互连在一起，这样整个建筑就像一个伸出地面的中空筒或者刚性盒子，这就是筒体结构，如图 6.5 所示。

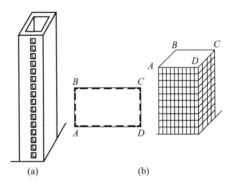

图 6.5　筒体结构

预应力混凝土结构　预应力混凝土是通过引入适合大小和分布的内部应力，来抵消由外部荷载所产生的应力的。在钢筋混凝土构件中，预应力通常由张拉钢筋来实现。预应力施加方法有先张法和后张法。

使用高强度材料可以减小预应力混凝土结构构件的截面尺寸，减少材料的自重，使更大跨度的结构在技术上和经济上可行。

2. 砌体结构

在中国最早使用的砌体可以追溯到两千多年前。在使用钢筋混凝土之前，砌体如石料、砖以及木材是主要的建筑材料。即使在现代，由于其较好的隔热性能并易于制造和施工，大多数国家特别是发展中国家正在使用它作为主要的住宅建筑材料。

砌体结构以其较低的成本在发展中国家有了很广泛的应用。但大家都知道，由于砌体材料如砖或砌块是一种脆性材料，其抗压能力强，但其拉伸能力弱，变形或延性都较差。房屋由延性材料建造可以承受严重的地震作用，并且即使发生严重破坏也不会倒塌，但那些使用脆性材料的房屋一旦遇到超过它们抵抗能力的严重地震作用时就会突然倒塌。因此，在那些可能会遇到严重地震的地方，必须有严格的条文来限制建造砌体房屋。

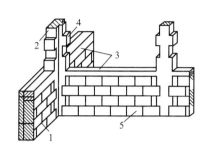

图 6.6　复合砌体结构
1—纵墙；2—构造柱；3—圈梁；4—马牙槎；5—横墙

已经研究出了几种先进的方法使抗震设防地区的砌体结构有延性，其中的一种就是复合砌体结构，如图 6.6 所示。即在砌体墙中嵌入小型的钢筋混凝土柱，并使柱和梁连接成对围护墙体的结构形式。钢筋混凝土柱的位置、尺寸、数量及钢筋的数量可由结构计算来确定。不像钢筋混凝土框架结构中的砌体填充墙，复合砌体结构中的砌体是在混凝土浇筑之前砌筑的。柱和梁浇筑之后，砌体墙和混凝土构件通过柱身上的马牙槎很好地连接在一起，并且在柱子和砌体墙连接的灰缝处放置水平拉结钢筋。这样，结构中的混凝土和砌体构件能够彼此相互限制，并能变形协调。由于相互限制的特性，所以命名这种钢筋混凝土柱为构造柱，梁为圈梁。在这种结构中，裂缝将会首先出现在砌体上，然后是混凝土柱，之后斜裂缝穿透砌体并且开始滑动。这种结构在中国被广泛地接受和使用。追踪调查表明，即使温度裂缝也很难在这样的结构中被发现，这就意味着该结构有良好的整体性。

最便宜的砌体材料是砖，它也是我国最广泛应用的材料。因为在早期的复合砌体研究中，主要的研究都集中在砖上。但是近些年来，为了保护土地资源和生态环境，中国政府鼓励人们使用节能材料，如用空心混凝土砌块来代替黏土砖。空心砌块在世界各地都被广泛应用，但在中国的应用却非常有限，每年的用量不到全部墙体材料的 1%。使用空心混凝土砌块至少有四大优点：①节约耕地（使用空心混凝土砌块代替黏土砖能节省超过 10000 公顷的土地）；②节约能源（空心混凝土砌块消耗的能源仅是黏土砖的 46%，如果半数的黏土砖能被空心混凝土砌块所代替，那么在中国将会节约 300 万吨原煤）；③减少 22%～40% 的建筑物自重，这样可以减少在地震中的地震力；④缩短建设工期并且节省超过 10% 的工程造价。这些优势表明混凝土空心砌块有着非常吸引人的应用前景。

3. 钢结构

钢结构是一种应用广泛的建筑结构形式，其中钢材发挥主导作用。钢材提供了较高的抗压和抗拉能力，并且使建筑物变得更轻。钢结构使用立体桁架，因此它们能实现比相应的混凝土结构更大的跨度。

Reading material Ⅰ

American Architecture

In 1883 a Chicago architect, W. L. B. Jenney, was asked to design an office building. Twenty-six years earlier the first American elevator had been installed in a New York building. Taking advantage of elevator transportation, Jenney designed the first skyscraper. It was originally ten stories high; two more stories were added later. Other tall elevator buildings soon followed.

In Jenney's office worked a young architect, Louis Sullivan, who became a leader of the opposition (反对) to the use of traditional styles in American architecture. Sullivan was not only a great architect but also a great philosopher. His building designs contributed to the development of modern architecture, and his writings influenced many young architects. He was deeply moved by the potential (潜在的) beauty of the skyscraper, which, he said, must be "a proud and soaring thing". Sullivan believed that the function of a building must determine its form and that practical needs must be the basis of an architect's planning and design.

In the years after 1900 Frank Lloyd Wright, a student of Sullivan, continued his teacher's rejection (抛弃) of traditional design. He had a deep belief in simplicity and in the importance of the unity (一致) of form and function. During his 66-years career, which lasted until his death in 1959, Wright designed houses, churches, museums, skyscrapers, and factories. His low, one-story houses established many features of contemporary (当代的) house design, including the "carport (简陋的汽车棚)", which he invented and named. The carport is a roofed area, attached to the house and used as a shelter for an automobile. Wright was probably the most original and creative architect of his time.

The important new architecture of the early twentieth century was the modern skyscraper. By the 1930s these towering building reached their greatest height in the Empire State Building, which rises 102 stories and 1250 feet (381m). The Empire State Building remained the tallest skyscraper in the world for 41 years.

Skyscrapers seemed particularly suitable for large cities, where land was expensive and tall buildings offered the most efficient use of space. Some cities, however, have limited the number of floors that a building may have. Washington D. C., for example, prohibits the construction of buildings more than 13 stories high. It is felt that skyscrapers would spoil the appearance (外观) of the city and the government buildings. In recent years, architects have designed somewhat lower structures and have given attention to light and open space. Many post-World War II skyscrapers feature what have been called glass-curtain walls. Entire (整个的) walls of these tall buildings are made of panes of glass. However, with the increasing concern (担心) over the declining (下降) supply of energy sources, many architects are turning away from this emphasis on glass. They are looking for building materials and designs that will require less air conditioning in hot weather and less artificial heat in cold weather.

The Empire State Building

The last several years have seen renewed interest in the construction of very tall skyscrapers. The World Trade Center in New York was completed in the early 1970s. It consists of twin towers, each 1350 feet high, with lobbies (门厅) seven stories high and 55 passenger elevators. It was attacked by terrorists (恐怖分子) on the day of 9/11/2001. The Sears Tower, a new Chicago skyscraper, has 110 stories, and the distance to the roof is 1454 feet (443m).

There is considerable debate in the architectural world about the future of such towering buildings. Many critics reject them as uneconomical and inefficient. Others reject skyscrapers devoted only to office space. They think that future skyscrapers should also provide living areas for those who work in the city.

Many modern urban and suburban apartment houses have adapted skyscraper architecture to contemporary (当代的) living. Known as "high-rise" buildings, they use many families in single buildings or groups of buildings. Apartments in these buildings are often equipped with such conveniences as air conditioning and various electric kitchen appliances such as clothes washing and drying machines and automatic waste disposers. Some apartment houses even contain small grocery stores for convenient shopping.

The World Trade Center   The Sears Tower

Reading material Ⅱ

Taiwan, a Beautiful Island Province of China

Taiwan is an island province of China. It is made up of fourteen islands of the Taiwan group and sixty-four islands of the Penghu group. The principal island of Taiwan has a coastline of about one thousand miles. It is about two hundred and forty miles long and ninety miles wide and has an area of about 13,500 square miles. It is separated from the mainland by the Taiwan Strait, which is only ninety miles across at its narrowest spot.

Our ancestors (祖先) knew of Taiwan as early as the seventh century B.C. By 1,500, many Chinese nationalities had settled there. In the seventeenth century the Dutch rulers set up trading settlements on the island. In 1661 an army under General Zheng Cheng gong drove out the Dutch (荷兰人). The government of the Qing Dynasty occupied Taiwan in 1683 and ruled it for over two centuries.

After the Sino-Japanese War of 1894—1895. Taiwan was ceded (割让) to Japan. Only after Japan was defeated in World War II was Taiwan returned to China and made a province by the Chinese government.

Lesson 7　Building Construction

Text

　　Building construction is a specialized branch of civil engineering concerned with the planning, execution and control of construction operations for such projects as highways, buildings, dams, airports, and utility lines.

　　Construction is the translation of a design to reality. The designer must be in close contact with everything that is done during the construction. The constructors should have the same building knowledge as the designer. More workers are employed during the peak period. They should be given training for working skills and knowledge about quality and safety as early as possible, so that they can work more efficiency.

　　The construction can be divided into some stages: evaluation, planning the job, preparation of site, earthmoving, foundation treatment, building the structure, tests on Completion and Employer's Taking-over.

　　Preparation of site　　This consists of the removal and clearing of all surface structures and growth from the site of the proposed structure. A bulldozer is used for small structures, larger structures must be dismantled.

　　Earthmoving　　This includes excavation and the placement of earth filling. Excavation follows preparation of the site, and is performed when the existing grade must be brought down to a new elevation. Excavation generally starts with the separate stripping of the organic topsoil, which is later reused for landscaping around the new building. This also prevents contamination of the inorganic material which is below the topsoil and which may be required for filling. Excavation may be done by any of several excavators (Fig 7.1), such as shovels, draglines, clamshells, cranes, and scrapers[1].

　　Efficient excavation on land requires a dry excavation area. Dewatering becomes a major operation when the excavation lies below the natural water table and intercepts the groundwater flow. When this occurs, dewatering and stabilizing of the soil may be accomplished by trenches, which conduct seepage to a sump from which the water is pumped out. Dewatering and stabilizing of the soil may in other cases be accomplished by well points and electroosmosis.

　　Some materials, such as rocks, cemented gravels, and hard clays, require blasting to loosen or fragment the material. Blast holes are drilled in the material; explosives are then placed in the blast holes and detonated. The quantity of explosives and the blast-hole spacing are dependent upon the type and structure of

(a) Shovels (b) draglines
(c) clamshells (d) scrapers

Fig 7.1 The Sketch Map of Several Excavators

the rock and the diameter and depth of the blast holes.

After placement of the earth fill, it is almost always compacted to prevent subsequent settlement. Compaction is generally done with sheep's-foot, grid, pneumatic-tired, and vibratory-type roller, which are towed by tractors over the fill as it is being placed. Hand-held, gasoline-driven rammers are used for compaction close to structures where there is no room for rollers to operate[2].

Foundation treatment When subsurface investigation reveals structural defects in the foundation area to be used for a structure, the foundation must be strengthened. Water passages, cavities, fissures, faults, and other defects are filled and strengthened by grouting. Grouting consists of injection of fluid mixtures under pressure. The fluids subsequently solidify in the voids of the strata. Most grouting is done with cement and water mixtures, but other mixture ingredients are asphalt, cement and clay, and precipitating chemicals.

Steel erection The construction of a steel structure consists of the assembly at the site of mill-rolled or shop-fabricated steel sections[3]. The steel sections may consist of beams, columns, or small trusses which are joined together by riveting, bolting, or welding. The crane is the most common type of erection equipment, but when a structure is too high or extensive in area to be erected by a crane, it is necessary to place one or more derricks on the structure to handle the steel. For river bridges the steel may be handled by cranes on barges, and if the bridge is too high, by traveling derricks which ride the bridge being erected. Cables for long suspension bridges are assembled in place by special equipment that pulls the wire from a reel, set up at one anchorage, across to the opposite anchorage, repeating the operation until the bundle of wires is of the required size[4].

Concrete construction   Concrete construction consists of several operations: forming, concrete production, placement, and curing (Fig 7.2). Forming is required to contain and support the fluid concrete within its desired final outline until it solidifies and can support itself.

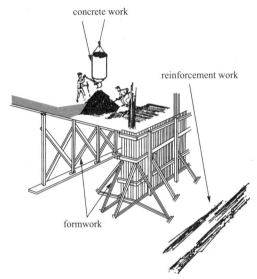

Fig 7.2   The Sketch Map of Concrete Construction

The usual practice for vertical walls is to leave the forms in position for at least one day after the concrete is placed. They are removed when the concrete has solidified or set. Slip-forming is a method where the form is constant in motion (Fig 7.3), just ahead of the level of fresh concrete.

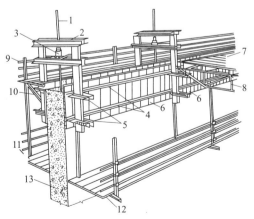

Fig 7.3   The Sketch Map of Slip-forming

1—support bar; 2—elevator; 3—hydraulic jack; 4—rib; 5—rib supporting; 6—framework;
7—operation table; 8—truss of table; 9—railing; 10—external tripod;
11—external scaffold cradle; 12—internal scaffold; 13—concrete wall

Concrete may be obtained from commercial batch plants which deliver it in mix trucks if the job is close to such a plant, or it may be produced at the job site.

Concrete is placed by cutting directly from the mixer truck (Fig 7.4), where possible, or from buckets handled by means of cranes or cableways, or it can be pumped into place by special concrete pumps.

Fig 7.4　The Sketch Map of Mixer Truck

Curing of exposed surfaces is required to prevent evaporation of mix water or to replace moisture that does evaporate. The proper balance of water and cement is required to develop full design strength.

Prestressed concrete construction: The common construction method of prestressed concrete is pre-tensioning and post-tensioning (Fig 7.5).

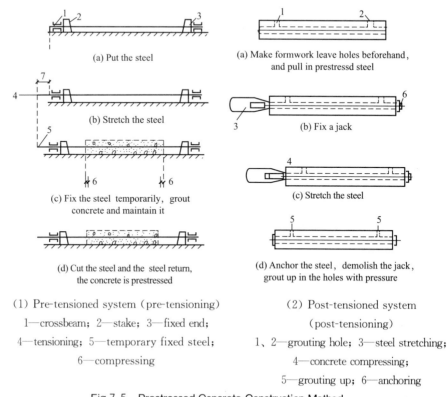

(a) Put the steel

(a) Make formwork leave holes beforehand, and pull in prestressd steel

(b) Stretch the steel

(b) Fix a jack

(c) Fix the steel temporarily, grout concrete and maintain it

(c) Stretch the steel

(d) Cut the steel and the steel return, the concrete is prestressed

(d) Anchor the steel, demolish the jack, grout up in the holes with pressure

(1) Pre-tensioned system (pre-tensioning)
1—crossbeam; 2—stake; 3—fixed end;
4—tensioning; 5—temporary fixed steel;
6—compressing

(2) Post-tensioned system
(post-tensioning)
1、2—grouting hole; 3—steel stretching;
4—concrete compressing;
5—grouting up; 6—anchoring

Fig 7.5　Prestressed Concrete Construction Method

Prestressed concrete use steels and concrete of very high. strength in combination. Prestressed concrete is particularly suited to prefabrication on mass-production basis, although it is being used as well without such prefabrication. Its introduction has extended to a very significant degree, the range of structural uses of the combination of these two materials.

Tests on completion and employer's taking-over The contractor shall carry out the test on completion after providing the As-Built Documents and Operation and Maintenance Manuals.

The contractor shall give to the engineer not less than 21 days' notice of the date after which the contractor will be ready to carry out each of the tests on completion. Unless otherwise agreed, tests on completion shall be carded out within 14 days after this date, on such day or days as the engineer shall instruct. Unless otherwise stated, the tests on completion shall be carried out in the following sequence:

(1) Pre-commissioning tests.

(2) Commissioning tests.

(3) Trial operation.

If the works, or a section, fail to pass the tests on completion, the engineer or the contractor may require the failed tests, and tests on completion and any related work, to be repeated under the same terms and conditions.

New Words and Phrases

1.	execution	[ˌeksɪˈkjuːʃn]	实行,实施,施工
2.	bulldozer	[ˈbʊldəʊzə(r)]	推土机,开土机,压路机
3.	dismantle	[dɪsˈmæntl]	拆除,拆卸,粉碎
4.	shovel	[ˈʃʌvl]	铲,挖掘机,单斗挖土机
5.	dragline	[ˈdræɡlaɪn]	拉索,拉铲挖土机
6.	clamshell	[ˈklæmʃel]	抓斗,蛤壳式挖泥机
7.	crane	[kreɪn]	起重机
8.	scraper	[ˈskreɪpə(r)]	铲运机,刮土机,平土机
9.	contamination	[kənˌtæmɪˈneɪʃn]	玷污,污染,污染物
10.	inorganic	[ˌɪnɔːˈɡænɪk]	无机的
11.	well point	[wel pɔɪnt]	降低地下水位的井点,深坑点
12.	electroosmosis	[ɪˌlektrəʊzˈməʊsɪs]	[物]电渗

13. fragment	[ˈfrægmənt]	断片，碎块，使成为碎片
14. detonate	[ˈdetəneɪt]	突然大爆炸，使爆炸
15. compact	[kəmˈpækt]	土体压实
16. grid	[grɪd]	格栅，格子
17. vibratory-type roller		振动碾
18. tow	[təʊ]	拖，拉，牵引
19. solidify	[səˈlɪdɪfaɪ]	固化，固结，凝固
20. ingredient	[ɪnˈgriːdɪənt]	组分，成分，配料
21. derrick	[ˈderɪk]	悬臂式起重机
22. asphalt	[ˈæsfælt]	沥青
23. strata	[ˈstrɑːtə]	stratum 的复数，层，地层，阶层
24. mixer truck	[ˈmɪksə trʌk]	混凝土搅拌车
25. prestressed concrete	[ˌpriːstrestˈkɒŋkriːt]	预应力混凝土
26. as built	[əz bɪlt]	建成的，竣工的
27. manual	[ˈmænjuəl]	手册，指南
28. precommissioning test	[priːkəˈmɪʃnɪŋ test]	启用前试验
29. commissioning test	[kəˈmɪʃnɪŋ test]	启用试验，试运行
30. prefabrication	[ˌpriːfæbrɪˈkeɪʃn]	预先制造
31. take over	[teɪkˈəʊvə]	接任，接管，验收

Notes

[1] Excavation may be done by any of several excavators, such as shovels, draglines, clamshells, cranes, and scrapers.

土体开挖可由下列任何一种开挖机械实施，如单斗挖土机、拉铲挖土机、抓铲挖土机、起重机、铲运机等。

[2] Compaction is generally done with sheep's-foot, grid, pneumatic-tired, and vibratory-type rollers, which are towed by tractors over the fill as it is being placed. Hand-held, gasoline-driven rammers are used for compaction close to structures where there is no room for rollers to operate.

土体压实常用羊足碾、平碾、气胎碾、振动碾压路机，由牵引机拖拉在回填土上进行碾压。当没有操作压路机的空间时，常用手持式煤油驱动锤来进行土体压实。

[3] The construction of a steel structure consists of the assembly at the site of mill-rolled or shop-fabricated steel sections.

钢结构施工包括现场轧制和预制装配两种。

[4] Cables for long suspension bridges are assembled in place by special equipment that pulls the wire from a reel, set up at one anchorage, across to

the opposite anchorage, repeating the operation until the bundle of wires is of the required size.

大跨度吊桥（悬索桥）装配施工是现场由特殊设备从一盘钢绞线上拉出钢丝固定在桥的一头，再拉到河对岸，固定在桥的另一头，如此反复数次，直至钢缆达到所需尺寸。

参考译文

第7课 建筑施工

建筑施工是土木工程的一个分支，主要包含公路、建筑物、水坝、机场和公共设施的设计、施工和施工过程控制。

建筑施工是将设计变成现实的过程。设计师必须密切关注施工过程中的所有事情。施工方应该像设计师一样有相同的建筑知识。在高峰期，会雇用大量的工人。他们应该尽早进行与质量和安全相关的技能和知识培训，以便使工作的效率更高。

建筑施工可被分为以下几个阶段：评估阶段，工作计划，场地准备，土方运输，基础处理，结构施工，竣工初验和雇主接收。

场地准备 包括所有已有地表结构物和将建建筑物会产生的垃圾的清理清除。对小型结构常用推土机清理，对大型结构必须拆除。

土方运输 包括土体开挖和回填土的处理。土体开挖紧接着场地平整，将原有的土体标高下降到合适的新标高。土体开挖通常以地表有机土的分层分离开始，分离出的土体常常被用于新建筑物的景观美化。同时要避免回填土时地表土下无机物的污染。土体开挖可由下列任何一种开挖机械实施（图7.1），如单斗挖土机、拉铲挖土机、抓铲挖土机、起重机、铲运机等。

有效地土体开挖要求有一个干燥的工作面。因此，排水成为开挖天然水平面下的土体和阻止地下水流动的主要施工过程。基坑排水和土体稳定可通过排水沟将地下水排至集水坑，再用水泵将水抽走。也可采用井点除水或电渗除水。

一些材料，比如岩石、水泥土碎石和硬黏土，要求爆破成松散结构或碎片，如在材料上钻孔，放置炸药、引爆。炸药的数量和炸药孔的间距由岩石的类型、结构和炸药孔的直径和深度而定。

土体回填后，常常进行土体压实以防止土体后期沉降。土体压实常用羊足碾、平碾、气胎碾、振动碾压路机，由牵引机拖拉在回填土上进行碾压。当没有操作压路机的空间时，常用手持式煤油驱动锤来进行土体压实。

地基处理 当地质勘查发现地基基础处有结构缺陷时，必须对地基进行加强处理。有水的道路、孔洞、裂缝、断层以及其他质量缺陷都可以通过注浆法进行填充和加固。常常是在压力下进行注浆加固，使注浆液在土层的空隙处逐渐固化。绝大多数注浆液是水泥浆，除此之外，沥青、水泥、黏土、速凝的化学浆也可用于地基加固。

(a) 单斗挖土机

(b) 拉铲挖土机

(c) 抓铲挖土机

(d) 铲运机

图 7.1　几种开挖机械示意图

钢结构安装　钢结构施工包括现场轧制和预制装配两种。钢结构部件包括钢梁、钢柱或小桁架，通过铆接、螺栓连接或焊接连接成整体。起重机是最常见的安装设备，但当建筑物太高或安装面积太大时，就有必要设置一个或多个悬臂起重机。钢架桥安装时在驳船上安装起重机，如果桥太高，应跨桥安装移动式悬臂起重机。大跨度吊桥（悬索桥）装配施工是现场由特殊设备从一盘钢绞线上拉出钢丝固定在桥的一头，再拉到河对岸，固定在桥的另一头，如此反复数次，直至钢缆达到所需尺寸。

混凝土施工　混凝土施工包括混凝土的成形、拌制、浇注和养护（图 7.2）。模板施工要求模板能在混凝土凝固和产生强度之前支撑液体混凝土。

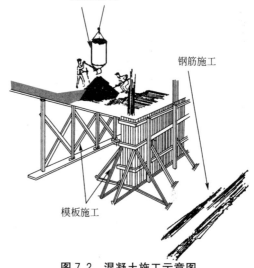

图 7.2　混凝土施工示意图

通常，竖向混凝土墙模板至少在混凝土浇筑完一天凝结固化后，才能拆除。滑模施工是一种使模板不断运动，模板始终在新浇混凝土面上部的一种施工方法(图7.3)

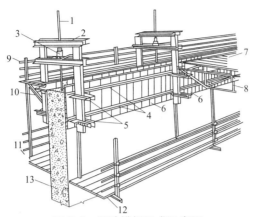

图7.3 滑动模板组成示意图

1—支承杆；2—提升架；3—液压千斤顶；4—围圈；5—围圈支柱；6—模板；7—操作平台；8—平台桁架；9—栏杆；10—外排三脚架；11—外吊脚手；12—内吊脚手；13—混凝土墙体

混凝土可由厂家生产用混凝土搅拌车运输到施工现场，或在施工现场现场制作。

混凝土可直接从混凝土搅拌车(图7.4)中沿斜槽下滑就位或通过起重机或沿空中索道用铲斗运输，也可以通过特殊的混凝土泵运输。

图7.4 混凝土搅拌车示意图

混凝土养护要求防止暴露在外的混凝土表面蒸发水分，或使蒸发掉的水分及时得以补充。为使混凝土完全达到设计强度，合理的水灰比是必需的。

预应力混凝土施工：常用的预应力混凝土施工方法有先张法和后张法两种(图7.5)。

预应力混凝土综合利用了高强钢筋和高强混凝土。虽然非工厂预制的预应力混凝土也被人们使用，但预应力钢筋混凝土最适于工厂预制和大批量生产，预应力混凝土的利用在很大程度上扩展了两种材料结合使用的范围。

竣工初验和雇主的接收　承包商应该在提交了《竣工文件》与《操作和维修手册》后，进行竣工初验。

承包商应该至少提前21天将其可以进行某项竣工初验的日期通知工程师。

除非另有商定，竣工初验应在该日期之后的 14 天内，在工程师指定的某日或某几日进行。除非另有说明，竣工初验应按下列顺序进行：

（1）启动前初验。

（2）启动初验。

（3）试运行。

如果工程或某一分项工程没有能够通过竣工初验，工程师或承包商可以要求按照相同的条款和条件，重新进行这项未通过的试验和相关工程的竣工初验。

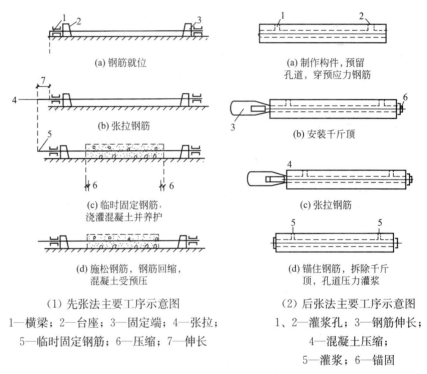

(1) 先张法主要工序示意图
1—横梁；2—台座；3—固定端；4—张拉；
5—临时固定钢筋；6—压缩；7—伸长

(2) 后张法主要工序示意图
1、2—灌浆孔；3—钢筋伸长；
4—混凝土压缩；
5—灌浆；6—锚固

图 7.5 预应力混凝土施工方法

Reading material Ⅰ

Building Construction

Building methods and materials throughout the world are more alike now than in the past. New blocks of offices or flats often look similar wherever they are built. Building a new home or office can take a long time. Much work has to be done before construction can start.

A person or company that wishes to put up a building must first have a plan made of it. This job is done by an architect. His plans show exactly what the new building will look like. An architect is part engineer and part artist. He must make calculations to be sure that his building will stay up when it is built. He has to know how strong the materials are that he wants to use. He must work out the weight that will press on the walls and floors when the building is in use. Only then can he be certain that no part of his building will be overloaded (超载) and that the whole structure will be safe.

The architect also tries to make the building look as attractive as possible and designs it so that it fits in with surrounding buildings. He must make sure that the building will be pleasant and comfortable to live and work in. He must also make sure that it will not cost too much to build.

The architect's plans must be approved by the local planners before work can start. The builders begin by digging down into the ground to make foundations for the building. The foundations go down beneath (在下面) the building and secure (保证) it firmly (坚固地) in the ground. The builders also lay pipes for drainage (排水) and water supply, and other services such as electricity and gas.

If a tall building is being built, the next job is to build a frame of steel or concrete on the foundations. A crane (起重机) is used to lift the heavy girders (刚架) or beams into their positions. Workmen, who must have a good head for height (不怕攀高), then fix them together. Floors and walls are lifted up and fixed on. They are often concrete slabs which are made in a factory and brought to the site. Sometimes a tall building uses the core (核心) to house the lift shaft (井筒). Then each storey (floor) is built around the core.

Next the roof and staircases are constructed so that workmen can work inside the shell of the building. They install wires and pipes for the various services. They fit windows, doors, wall panels (墙板), ceilings, floor coverings, and all kinds of other fittings (设备). Then decorators (装饰工人) complete the building and it is ready for its first occupiers (住户).

Reading material II

The Lugou Bridge, One of the Best-known Arched Bridges in China

The Lugou Bridge, also known as the Marco Polo Bridge, was built in 1189 on the southwestern outskirts (郊外) of Beijing.

Considered to be one of the best-known arched bridges in China, the bridge is 266.5 meters long, 7.5 meters wide and it has 11 arches and 140 stone columns. "It is indeed the most wonderful and unique bridge in the world," wrote the Italian traveler Marco Polo in his book Travels of Marco Polo. So the Lugou Bridge is one of the city's famous historic sites.

Besides the outstanding architecture, what interests people most about the Lugou Bridge is the stone lions carved on the columns. The lions are extremely lifelike (栩栩如生). Each column is topped with a big lion surrounded by many smaller ones, and the smallest is only a few centimeters high. Some of them stand on the heads or backs of the bigger ones, some lie under their feet or in their embrace, and others show only half a head, only a mouth. Vivid (生动的) and lively, they are depicted (展现) in different postures—sitting, lying, standing and crouching.

As the natives of Beijing put it, the stone lions on the Lugou Bridge are too many to be counted. The stories about them are also most interesting. One says that one of the lions is always swimming so that it is impossible to count the lions exactly because some are hidden and can't be seen, and that if an exact count were really made all the lions would run away.

True, nobody could have kept count of them. It was not until 1961 that the cultural offices discovered their exact number as altogether four hundred and eighty-five.

Lesson 8 Engineering Construction Supervision

Text

Engineering construction supervision is a technology - intensive and intelligent work, involving the construction of a variety of professional and academic knowledge and a wealth of knowledge about knowledge management, legal and economic minds[1]. With the development of the construction market, engineering construction supervision has become inevitable, which is a very good help and supervision of the construction manager. For investment decisions, benefits and specifications of the project construction participation conduct, project quality and safety has played an extremely important role[2].

Construction supervision in China started in 1988, has been thirty years now. At present, the construction market in China has formed a project management, owners, and contractors construction of three equal and independent bodies[3]. As a project management unit, should pay attention to "quality, progress and investment in" three controls, and as project coordinator and manager of the most important in the construction, coordinate relationships with owners, construction units, to ensure that construction is scheduled for "quality, investment and progress goals" implementation[4].

1. To raise the level of scientific construction project investment decision

Construction project investment amounts are generally large, millions of, tens of millions, billions of. Such a large investment it is directly related to major economic interests of national, industry, regional, and national economy, so the decision should be wary. However, at this time, construction engineering supervision appeared, it is a great help. It can help the construction units to select an appropriate engineering consultancy, based on the results of the consultation (such as the project proposal and feasibility study report, which evaluate modifications made valuable comments and suggestions). It can also be directly for the construction units to provide the construction program[5]. Adequately address the construction units of concern. Since the beginning of this, makes investments in line with the national economic development planning, industrial policy, investment and invest more in line with market demand, avoiding the blind and irrational investment, also to avoid unjustified losses from investments, bringing the Gospel to the State and people.

2. In favour of regulating the behavior of project construction of participating parties

Since construction is a multi‐party participation completed in a collaborative process. Participation and all parties will stand in their thinking, and combined with the self interest, it does appear and run counter to the construction of engineering quality behavior. Therefore, simply depending on market laws, regulations, rules and criteria that is not enough, It should be done by an organization to supervise, it is construction engineering supervision enterprises. And its supervision and constraint mechanism of compulsory feature, participation have to code for its constraints and under the supervision of the job. In the process of implementation of the construction project, supervision of engineering project management enterprise pursuant to delegated contracts and construction contracts related to construction supervision and management of the Contracting Unit. Because of this constraint mechanisms throughout the whole process of project construction, used prior, and the combination of ex-post controls, so you can effectively regulate the Contracting Unit construction, minimize improper construction behavior[6].

3. Conducive to the Contracting unit to ensure construction quality and safety

The direct implementation of unit construction is the construction, are the key to quality to guarantee and safeguard people's life and property safety, health and the environment. Building works as a special type of product, not allowing any slack and negligent in this regard. And due to so, special needs engineering supervision enterprise to on contractors units of construction behavior implementation strong of supervision management, led contractors units in construction process in the strictly by figure construction, and strictly seriously job each road process, and do since correcting self and ultimate check phase combination, and to this strengthening on engineering quality of implementation and management, reached design quality of requirements, and meet products needs who of requirements, to ensure engineering of quality and using security.

4. Conducive to the realization of investment construction project maximized benefits

Huge amounts of a construction project investment, investment in both countries, and also private individuals and even financing, funding late effect will directly affect the country's economic development, social progress, peace and harmony. Therefore only making investments paying dividends, is the real investment; To maximize the investment, returns that is sensible and ideal subject of investment. Construction project investment is to meet the intended function and construction projects under the premise of quality standards, investment of at least; to meet the intended function and construction projects under the premise of quality standards, project life cycle cost (or life cycle costs) at least; construction works of investment efficiency is to maximize the environmental and social benefits of comprehensive benefits[7]. Only so as to realize the significance of investment, and achieve the purpose of project management.

New Words and Phrases

1. supervision   [ˌsjuːpəˈvɪʒn]   监督；管理
2. intelligent   [ɪnˈtelədʒənt]   聪明的；理解力强的；有智力的
3. inevitable   [ɪnˈevɪtəbl]   不可避免的；必然发生的
4. dozen   [ˈdʌzən]   (一)打，十二个
5. regional   [ˈriːdʒənl]   地区的，区域的
6. appropriate   [əˈprəʊprɪət]   适当的；恰当的；合适的
7. modification   [ˌmɒdɪfɪˈkeɪʃn]   修改，修正，变更，改良
8. enterprise   [ˈentərpraɪz]   事业，计划；事业心，进取心
9. criteria   [kraɪˈtɪrɪə]   标准，准则
10. oversight   [ˈəʊvəsaɪt]   监督，照管；失察；负责
11. constraint   [kənˈstrent]   强制；限制；约束
12. mechanism   [ˈmekənɪzəm]   机制，机能
13. compulsory   [kəmˈpʌlsərɪ]   必须做的，强制性的；义务的；必修
14. pursuant   [pəˈsjuːənt]   追踪的；依据的
15. guarantee   [ˌgærənˈtiː]   保证；担保；保障；保证书
16. negligent   [ˈneglɪdʒənt]   疏忽的；粗心大意的；懒散
17. commissioner   [kəˈmɪʃənə(r)]   专员；委员；长官

Notes

[1] Engineering construction supervision is a technology-intensive and intelligent work, involving the construction of a variety of professional and academic knowledge and a wealth of knowledge about knowledge management, legal and economic minds.

工程建设监理工作是技术密集型的、智能型的工作，涉及建筑业的多种专业和学科的相关知识及丰富的管理知识、法律知识及经济头脑。

[2] For investment decisions, benefits and specifications of the project construction participation conduct project quality and safety have played an extremely important role.

为工程项目的投资决策、效益及规范工程参建各方行为、工程质量与安全起到了极其重要的作用。

[3] At present, the construction market in China has formed a project management, owners, and contractors construction of three equal and independent bodies.

目前,我国的建筑市场已基本形成了监理、业主和承包商三大平等、独立的工程建设主体。

[4] As a project management unit, should pay attention to "quality, progress and investment in" three controls, and as project coordinator and manager of the most important in the construction, coordinate relationships with owners, construction units, to ensure that construction is scheduled for "quality, investment and progress goals" implementation.

作为监理单位,既要重视"质量、进度、投资"三大控制,又要作为工程建设中最主要的协调者和管理者,协调好与业主、施工单位之间的关系,以确保工程建设预定的"质量、投资、进度目标"的实现。

[5] It can help both the construction units to select an appropriate engineering consultancy, and on the results of the consultation (if the project proposal and feasibility study report) evaluate modifications made valuable comments and suggestions; can also be directly for the construction units to provide the construction program.

它既能够协助建设单位选择一个适合的工程咨询机构,并对咨询结果(如项目建议书、可行性研究报告)进行评估,提出有价值的修改意见和建议;也能够由自己直接为建设单位提供建设方案。

[6] Because of this constraint mechanisms throughout the whole process of project construction, used prior, and the combination of ex-post controls, so you can effectively regulate the Contracting unit construction, minimize improper construction behavior.

由于这种约束机制贯穿于工程建设的全过程,采用事前、事中和事后控制相结合的方式,因此可以有效地规范各承建单位的建设行为,最大限度地避免不当建设行为的发生。

[7] Construction project investment to meet the intended function and construction projects under the premise of quality standards, investment of at least; to meet the intended function and construction projects under the premise of quality standards, project life cycle cost (or life cycle costs) at least; construction works of investment efficiency and maximize the environmental and social benefits of comprehensive benefits.

即建设工程投资要在满足建设工程预定功能和质量标准的前提下,让投资额最少;在满足建设工程预定功能和质量标准的前提下,建设工程寿命周期费用(或全寿命费用)最少;建设工程本身的投资效益与环境、社会效益的综合效益最大化。

参 考 译 文

第8课　工程建设监理

工程建设监理工作是技术密集型的、智能型的工作,涉及建筑业的多种专业和学科的相关知识及丰富的管理知识、法律知识及经济头脑。随着建筑市场的发展,工程建设监理的产生成为必然,它是工程建设的一个很好协助者、监督管理者。为工程项目的投资决策、效益及规范工程参建各方行为、工程质量与安全起到了极其重要的作用。

我国工程建设监理自1988年起步,至今已有三十年了。目前,我国的建筑市场已基本形成了监理、业主和承包商三大平等、独立的工程建设主体。作为监理单位,既要重视"质量、进度、投资"三大控制,又要作为工程建设中最主要的协调者和管理者,协调好与业主、施工单位之间的关系,以确保工程建设预定的"质量、投资、进度目标"的实现。

1. 提高建设工程投资决策科学化的水平

建设工程投资数额一般都比较大,少则几百万,多则上千万、数十亿。这样大的投资直接关系到国家、行业、地区的重大经济利益,以及国计民生,因而在决策上应慎之又慎。然而,在这时,建设工程监理出现了,它就是一个很好的协助者。它既能够协助建设单位选择一个适合的工程咨询机构,并对咨询结果(如项目建议书、可行性研究报告)进行评估,提出有价值的修改意见和建议,也能够由自己直接为建设单位提供建设方案,充分解决建设单位的忧虑。如此一来,就能让投资符合国家的经济发展规划、产业政策、投资方向和项目投资更加符合市场需求,避免了盲目的、不合理的投资,也避免了不合理投资带来的损失,给国家和人民带来了福音。

2. 规范工程建设参与各方的建设行为

由于工程建设是一个多方参与、共同完成的一个协作过程,加之参建各方均会站在自己的角度思考行事以及利益的驱使,难免会出现与工程质量相违背的建设行为。因此,仅仅依赖法律、法规、规章和市场准则是远远不够的。所以,还需要有一个组织机构来完成实施监督,它就是建设工程监理企业。而且它的监督具有强制的约束机制的特点,让参建各方不得不在其约束与监督下规范作业。在建设工程实施过程中,工程监理企业可依据委托监理合同和有关的建设工程合同对承建单位的建设行为进行监督管理。由于这种约束机制贯穿于工程建设的全过程,采用事前、事中和事后控制相结合的方式，因此可以有效地规范各承建单位的建设行为，最大限度地避免不当建设行为的发生。

3. 促使承建单位保证建设工程质量和使用安全

承建单位是建筑工程的直接实施者，是质量得以保障的关键者，也是人民生命财产安全、健康和环境的捍卫者。所以建筑工程作为一种特殊的产品，不允许在这方面有丝毫的懈怠和疏忽。正因如此，特别需要工程监理企业来对承建单位的建设行为实施强有力的监督管理，促使承建单位在建设过程中严格按图施工、严格认真作业每一道工序，做到自纠自查与终极检查相结合，以此加强对工程质量的实施与管理，达到设计质量的要求，并满足产品需求者的要求，从而确保工程质量和使用安全。

4. 实现建设工程投资效益最大化

一项建设工程投资一般数额巨大，不论是国家投资，还是私企个体投资，甚至各种方式融资，资金产生的后期效应，都将直接影响到国家的经济发展，社会的进步、安宁与和谐。故而只有让投资产生效益，才是真正的投资；使投资效益最大化才是理智、理想符合发展的投资。即建设工程投资要在满足建设工程预定功能和质量标准的前提下，让投资额最少；在满足建设工程预定功能和质量标准的前提下，建设工程寿命周期费用（或全寿命费用）最少；建设工程本身的投资效益与环境、社会效益的综合效益最大化。只有这样才能实现投资的意义，达到工程监理的目的。

Reading material Ⅰ

How to control project quality

The rapid development of the economy for the construction market of our country has provided a broad space for development, but also for building participation parties put forward higher requirements. Engineering quality（工程质量）directly related to the engineering application（应用），not only with the enterprise's economic benefits（经济效益），but also with social economic benefit, ecological benefit closely related, affecting the development of numerous enterprise. China's construction industry norms continues to improve as well as regulatory strength increase ceaselessly, supervision company how to effectively carry out the supervision work, through the construction supervision and improving the quality control of construction process（施工过程），improve the quality of the project, for our country construction supervision development and lay a good foundation has become the primary problem of supervision enterprise.

1. Our country construction stage supervision status: at present our country construction stage supervision mainly through the supervision enterprise on-site supervision personnel（现场监理人员）. Along with the

quantity increase and the project is increasing, as a result of inspect manage personnel experience imbalance and staffing problems often leads to the construction stage supervision is not in place waiting to happen, can effectively guarantee the construction quality of engineering supervision to the engineering quality, bury (埋下) next hidden trouble (隐患). In view of this situation, how to effectively carry out the construction supervision, make full use of modern science and technology method to improve the supervision effect, promote the construction and improve the quality of our country has become the biggest problem facing (面临) the supervision enterprise. Supervision enterprises should through the procedures of supervision, standardization management (标准化管理) and the application of computer technology to promote the construction supervision work effectively, improve the supervision effect.

2. Engineering quality control during construction features: the project construction process quality control is characterized by the characteristics of the project decision. The project is one of the characteristics of single. The project is in accordance with the construction unit construction the intention of the design, the construction management of internal and external conditions, the construction site of the natural and social environment (环境), the production process each are not identical.

3. In the course of construction quality control supervision of principles: engineering quality control in construction process characteristics require us to construction quality control in supervision to follow certain principles, so as to ensure effective supervision work. 1, Adhere to the quality first (质量第一), giving priority to prevention; 2, adhere to quality standards; 3, adhere to the people oriented core (以人为本).

4. Strengthening the construction process quality control supervision: to strengthen the construction process quality control supervision, should be based on dynamic control beforehand prevention, supplemented by management methods, focusing on good guidance, in-process inspection, after the acceptance of three links, ahead of pre-control, from the angle of active control problem is found, on key parts, the dynamic control process and key, catch a key part of quality control for engineering construction, to whole process, all-around quality control, thereby effectively realize the overall quality control of project construction.

Reading material Ⅱ

Comfort and Discomfort

One of the goals of the environmental engineers and architects is to ensure comfortable conditions in a building. Thermal（热量的）pleasure can only be achieved locally over part of the body or temporarily in the context of a situation which is itself unacceptable. Continuous thermal pleasure extending over a period of hours is not possible. We are left simply with the idea of comfort as a lack of discomfort; this may seem an uninspiring（不令人激动的）definition（定义）, but nevertheless it presents real practical challenge.

General thermal discomfort will be felt if a person is either too hot or too cold. In addition there are several potential sources of local discomfort, such as cold feet or draught.

Any guide to comfort must relate these forms discomfort to the physical variables of the environment, so that a permissible（可以允许的）range of the variables may be recommended. It is conventional to treat overall discomfort in terms of thermal sensation.

It is clear, however, that their comfort rating cannot be transferred to the different situation. The standards of acceptability are set by the range of stimuli that people are used to. Poulton (1977) pointed out that this implies that the goal of providing a universally acceptable environment may be ever receding. If people do make judgments of acceptability on the basis of their own experience, then the maximum acceptable level will fall as the general level falls. If the noise level in a district is reduced, the level at which noise becomes unacceptable will also be reduced and so the loudest noise will always be too loud. Air conditioning engineers are often heard to complain that standards of expectation rise as fast as the standards of air conditioning, so that the level of complaints stays constant.

Lesson 9 Project Management

Text

Project management is the art of directing and coordinating human and material resources throughout the life of a project by using modern management techniques to achieve predetermined objectives of scope, cost, time, and quality.

Construction schedules In addition to assigning dates to project activities, project scheduling is intended to match resources of equipment, materials and labor with project work tasks over time. For example, Fig 9.1, the construction schedules of reinforced concrete precast pile. Good scheduling can eliminate problems due to production bottlenecks, facilitate the timely procurement of necessary materials, and otherwise insure in considerable waste as laborers and equipment wait for the availability of needed resources or the completion of preceding tasks. Delays in the completion of an entire project due to poor scheduling can also create havoc for owners who are eager to start using the constructed facilities[1].

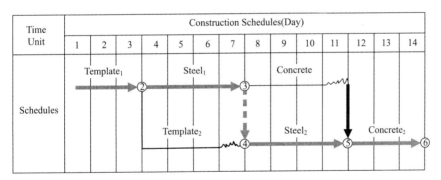

Fig 9.1 The Construction Schedules of Reinforced Concrete Precast Pile

Formal scheduling procedures have become much more common with the advent of personal computers on construction sites and easy-to-use software programs. Sharing scheduling information via the internet has also provided a greater incentive to use formal scheduling methods. Savvy construction supervisors often carry schedule and budget information around with wearable or handheld computers. As a result, the continued development of easy-to-use computer programs and improved methods of presenting schedules have overcome the practical problems associated with formal scheduling mechanisms. But problems with the use of scheduling techniques will continue until managers understand their proper use and limitations.

A basic distinction exists between resource-oriented and time-oriented scheduling techniques. For resource-oriented scheduling, the focus is on using and scheduling particular resources in an effective fashion. For time-oriented scheduling, the emphasis is on determining the completion time of resource leveling or resource constrained scheduling in the presence of precedence relationships also exist. Most scheduling software is time-oriented, although virtually all of the programs have the capability to introduce resource constraints.

Construction cost control Cost estimating is one of the most important steps in project management. A cost estimate establishes the base line of the project cost at different stages of development of the project. A cost estimate at a given stage of project development represents a prediction provided by the cost engineer or estimator on the basis of available data[2]. According to the American Association of Cost Engineers, cost engineering is defined as that area of engineering practice where engineering judgment and experience are utilized in the application of scientific principles and techniques to the problems of cost estimation, cost control and profitability.

A unit cost is assigned to each of the facility components or tasks as represented by the bill of quantities. The total cost is the summation of the products of the quantities multiplied by the corresponding unit cost. The unit cost method is straightforward in principle but quite laborious in application. The initial step is to break down or disaggregate a process into a number of tasks. Collectively, these tasks must be completed for the construction of a facility. Once these tasks are defined and quantities representing these tasks are assessed, a unit cost is assigned to each and then the total cost is determined by summing the cost incurred in each task[3]. The level of detail in decomposing into tasks will vary considerably from one estimate to another.

Construction quality control Quality control in construction typically involves insuring compliance with minimum standards of materials and workmanship in order to insure the performance of the facility according to the design[4]. For the purpose of insuring compliance, random samples and statistical methods are commonly used as the basis for accepting or rejecting work completed and batches of materials. Rejection of a batch is based on nonconformance or violation of the relevant design specification.

An implicit assumption in these traditional quality control practices is the notion of an acceptable quality level which is a allowable fraction of defective items. Materials obtained from suppliers or work performed by an organization is inspected and passed as acceptable if the estimated defective percentage is within the acceptable quality level. Problems with materials or goods are corrected after delivery of the product.

In contrast to this traditional approach of quality control is the goal of total quality control. In this system, no defective items are allowed anywhere in the construction process. While the zero defect goal can never be permanently obtained, it provides a goal so that an organization is never satisfied with its quality control program even if defects are reduced by substantial amounts year after year. This concept and approach to quality control was first developed in manufacturing firms in Japan and Europe, but has since spread to many construction companies. The best known formal certification for quality improvement is the International Organization for Standardization's ISO 9000 standard[5]. ISO 9000 emphasizes good documentation, quality goals and a series of cycles of planning, implementation and review.

Total quality control is a commitment to quality expressed in all parts of an organization and typically involves many elements. Design reviews to insure safe and effective construction procedures are a major element. Other elements include extensive training for personnel, shifting the responsibility for detecting defects from quality control inspectors to workers, and continually maintaining equipment. Worker involvement in improved quality control is often formalized in quality circles in which groups of workers meet regularly to make suggestions for quality improvement. Material suppliers are also required to insure zero defect in delivered goods. Initially, all materials from a supplier are inspected and batches of goods with any defective items are returned. Suppliers with good records can be certified and not subject to complete inspection subsequently.

Of course, total quality control is difficult to apply, particular in construction. The unique nature of each facility, the variability in the workforce, the multitude of subcontractors and the cost of making necessary investments in education and procedures make programs of total quality control in construction difficult. Nevertheless, a commitment to improved quality even without endorsing the goal of zero defect can pay real dividends to organizations.

Example 9.1 Experience with Quality Circles

Quality circles represent a group of five to fifteen workers who meet on a frequent basis to identify, discuss and solve productivity and quality problems. A circle leader acts as liaison between the workers in the group and upper levels of management. Appearing below are some examples of reported quality circle accomplishments in construction.

(1) On a highway project under construction by ×× Corporation, it was found that the loss rate of ready-mixed concrete was too high. A quality circle

composed of cement masons found out that the most important reason for this was due to an inaccurate checking method. By applying the circle's recommendations, the loss rate was reduced by 11.4%.

(2) In a building project by ×× Construction Company, many cases of faulty reinforced concrete work were reported. The iron workers quality circle examined their work thoroughly and soon the faulty workmanship disappeared. A 10% increase in productivity was also achieved.

New Words and Phrases

1.	construction	[kənˈstrʌkʃn]	施工
2.	domain	[dəˈmeɪn]	领域
3.	aerospace	[ˈeərəʊspeɪs]	航天
4.	pharmaceutical	[ˌfɑːməˈsuːtɪkl]	医药的
5.	distinguish	[dɪˈstɪŋgwɪʃ]	区别，区分
6.	mission oriented	[ˈmɪʃn ˈɔːrɪəntɪd]	以目标（任务）为导向的
7.	predetermined	[ˌpriːdɪˈtɜːmɪnd]	预定的
8.	schedule	[ˈʃedjuːl]	进度
9.	production bottleneck	[prəˈdʌkʃn ˈbɒtlˌnek]	生产瓶颈
10.	havoc	[ˈhævək]	严重破坏
11.	constructed facilities	[kənˈstrʌktɪd fəˈsɪlɪtɪz]	建设设施
12.	construction schedules	[kənˈstrʌkʃn ˈʃedjuːəlz]	施工计划
13.	critical path method	[ˈkrɪtɪkəl pɑːθ ˈmeθəd]	关键线路法
14.	construction site	[kənˈstrʌkʃn saɪt]	工地
15.	budget	[ˈbʌdʒɪt]	预算
16.	resource oriented	[rɪˈsɔːs ˈɔːrɪəntɪd]	以资源为导向的
17.	hybrid technique	[ˈhaɪbrɪd tekˈniːk]	混合计划方法
18.	crane	[kreɪn]	起重机
19.	time oriented	[taɪm ˈɔːrɪəntɪd]	以时间为导向的
20.	cost estimation	[kɒst ˌestəˈmeɪʃən]	成本估算
21.	estimator	[ˈestɪmeɪtə]	估算师
22.	cost engineering	[kɒst ˈendʒɪˈnɪərɪŋ]	工程估价
23.	cost control	[kɒst kənˈtrəʊl]	成本控制
24.	bill of quantities	[bɪləv ˈkwɒntɪtɪz]	工程量清单

Notes

[1] Delays in the completion of an entire project due to poor scheduling can also create havoc for owners who are eager to start using the constructed facilities.

因为进度计划编排得不合理而造成整个项目完成时间的拖延会给急于使用建成设施的业主造成严重损失。

[2] A cost estimate at a given stage of project development represents a prediction provided by the cost engineer or estimator on the basis of available data.

在项目开发过程中的某一特定阶段的成本估算就是造价工程师在现有数据基础上对未来成本的预测。

[3] Once these tasks are defined and quantities representing these tasks are assessed, a unit cost is assigned to each and then the total cost is determined by summing the cost incurred in each task.

一旦这些任务确定下来，并有了工作量的估算，将单价与每项任务的工作量相乘就可以得到每项任务的成本。

[4] Quality control in construction typically involves insuring compliance with minimum standards of material and workmanship in order to insure the performance of the facility according to the design.

施工过程中的质量控制一般指保证材料和施工工艺符合最低标准，确保建成设施的功能达到设计要求。

[5] International Organization for Standardizations ISO 9000 standard

由国际标准化组织颁布的 ISO 9000 族质量体系认证标准。

参 考 译 文

第9课　工程项目管理

项目管理是在项目的整个周期内，用现代的管理技术指挥和协调人力和物质资源以取得成本、工期和质量等预定目标。

建筑施工进度计划　工程进度计划除了可以为各项活动安排日期外，还能够将工程全过程中用到的设备、材料和劳动力等各种资源进行合理的配备。图9.1所示为钢筋混凝土预制桩的进度计划。一个好的计划可以消除生产瓶颈带来的问题，同时也可以使各项必需的物资得以及时地采购，从而保证工程尽可能按时完工。相反，如果工程计划没有做好，则会在工程完成过程中造成窝工，对人工、设备等造成浪费。由于进度计划编排得不合理造成整个工期拖延，也会对急于使用建成设施的业主造成严重损失。

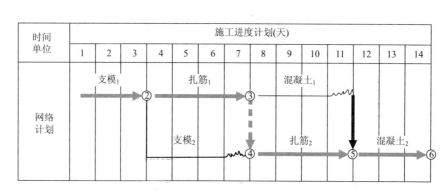

图 9.1 钢筋混凝土预制桩的施工进度计划

　　随着个人计算机在施工现场的出现以及易用的软件的问世,正规的计划编制已经变得比较普通了。通过因特网来分享工程计划信息也极大地促进了正式计划方法的使用,聪明的工程管理人员通常携带便携式计算机,并在里面存放工程计划和工程预算资料。事实上,易用的计算机软件的不断发展和现有计划方法的改进,已经解决了与正规计划手段有关的实际问题。但是,要解决与计划技术使用有关的问题,管理人员需要掌握并理解计划技术合理的使用方法及其局限性。

　　以资源为导向的计划编制法和以时间为导向的计划编制法之间有着明显的区别。对于以资源为导向的计划编制法来说,关键是如何运用有效的方式和那些特殊的资源来编制资源计划。对以时间为导向的计划编制法而言,重点是在给定各个活动之间的必要优先次序的情况下确定项目的完工时间。还有一种混合计划编制法,它是在确定2种优先关系之后进行的资源平衡或资源限制的计划编制法。大多数用来编制计划的软件都是时间计划编制软件,尽管它们实际上有能力引进资源限制计划编制法。

　　施工成本控制　成本估算是项目管理中最重要的环节之一。它在项目建设的不同阶段为项目的成本建立了一条基准线。在项目开发过程中的某一特定阶段的成本估算就是造价工程师在现有数据基础上对未来成本的预测。根据美国造价工程师协会的定义,工程估价是运用科学理论和技术,根据工程判断和经验,解决成本估算、成本控制和盈利能力等问题的活动。

　　由工程量清单表达的各项任务或各个组成部分的单位成本能够明确,总成本就是各项产品的数量与其相应单位成本的乘积之和。单位成本法虽然在理论上非常直接,但是难以应用。第一步是将某工作分解成许多项任务,当然每项任务都是为项目建设服务的。一旦这些任务确定,并有了工作量的估算,用单价与每项任务的量相乘就可以得到每项任务的成本,从而得到每项工作的总成本。当然,不同的估算中对每项工作分解的详细程度可能会有很大差别。

　　施工质量控制　施工过程中的质量控制是指保证材料和施工工艺符合最低标准,确保建筑设施达到设计要求的功能。为了确保符合标准,通常用随机抽样和数理统计方法作为接受或拒绝已完工作和批量材料的基础。所谓拒绝是指因质量不符合或违反了相关的设计标准而做出的决定。

在这些传统的质量控制实践中有一个隐含的假设——可接受的质量水平，它是指缺陷点的允许比例。来自供应商的材料或某个组织完成的工作只有当其缺陷比例在允许的质量水平以内时，才算合格并通过检查。在这种情况下，材料或产品存在的问题只能在交付后才能得以改正。

而与这个传统的质量控制方法相对照的则是全面质量控制的概念。在这个体系里，施工过程中的任何地方都不允许出现缺陷项目。尽管零缺陷这个目标是永远没有办法达到的，但它却为组织提供了一个目标，使得组织对其质量控制计划从不满足，即使缺陷项目逐年都有显著的降低。这种质量控制的概念和方法首先在日本和欧洲的一些制造企业当中得到发展，然后迅速普及到建筑公司。对于质量改进最为权威的认证是国际标准化组织的 ISO 9000 标准族。ISO 9000 标准族着重于质量文件、质量目标以及一系列计划、执行和检查的循环程序。

全面质量控制是组织的所有部分对质量的一个承诺，它通常包括很多要素，用以保证施工过程安全有效的设计评审工作就是一个主要因素。其他一些因素还包括广泛的人员培训，把发现缺陷的责任从检查者转移到操作者身上，以及持续地对设备进行维护等工作。在质量圈当中有一个正式的有关工人对质量控制改进的环节，即工人们定期会面并就质量改进提出建议。材料供应商在提供产品时，也保证零缺陷。起初，供应商的所有材料都要被抽检，而有缺陷的批次会被退回。有良好记录的供应商可以经核准免去进行全项检验。

诚然，全面质量控制的运用也绝非易事，尤其是在建筑施工中。每一项建筑产品都具有独一无二的特征，劳动力的不稳定性、分包商的多样性以及在教育和程序上的必要支出都使得在建筑施工中开展全面质量控制计划显得困难重重。尽管如此，即使没有达到零缺陷目标，对于质量改进的承诺也会使组织受益匪浅。

例 9.1　质量圈经验

质量圈小组通常由 5 至 15 个操作工人组成，他们定期开会以识别、讨论和解决生产率及质量问题。质量圈小组的领导则在操作工人和上层管理之间起着联络作用。下面是施工中质量圈小组的一些成功的例子。

(1) 由××公司承建的某高速公路项目，人们发现其商品混凝土的不合格率非常高，由混凝土工组成的质量圈小组经调查后发现造成这种现象的主要原因是检查方法不当。在采纳了该小组的建议后，不合格率下降了 11.4%。

(2) 由××建设公司承建的某住宅项目，经报告混凝土存在不足的事情时有发生。钢筋工质量圈小组在详细检查了他们的工作之后，找出了问题的原因，并将劳动生产率提高了 10%。

Reading material Ⅰ

Major Types of Construction

Since owners are generally interested in acquiring only a specific type of constructed facility(设备), they should be aware of the common industrial practices for the type of construction pertinent to them. Likewise, the construction industry is a conglomeration(集团) of quite diverse(不同的) segments(部门) and products. Some owners may procure(采购) a constructed facility only once in a long while and tend to look for short term advantages. However, many owners require periodic acquisition(定期采购) of new facilities and/or rehabilitation of existing facilities. It is to their advantage to keep the construction industry healthy and productive. Collectively, the owners have more power to influence the construction industry than they realize because, by their individual actions, they can provide incentives(鼓励) or disincentives for innovation efficiency and quality in construction. It is to the interest of all parties that the owners take an active interest in the construction and exercise beneficial influence on the performance of the industry.

In planning for various types of construction, the methods of procuring professional services, awarding construction contracts, and financing(负担经费) the constructed facility can be quite different. For the purpose of discussion, the broad spectrum(系列) of constructed facilities may be classified into four major categories, each with its own characteristics.

Residential housing construction Residential housing construction includes single-family houses, multi-family dwellings, and high-rise apartments. During the development and construction of such projects, the developers or sponsors(主办方) who are familiar with the construction industry usually serve as surrogate(代理人) owners and take charge, making necessary contractual agreements for design and construction, and arranging the financing and sale of the completed structures. Residential housing designs are usually performed by architects and engineers, and the construction executed by builders who hire subcontractors(承包商) for the structural, mechanical, electrical and other specialty work. An exception to this pattern is for single-family.

Institutional and commercial building construction Institutional and commercial building construction encompasses(包含) a great variety of project types and sizes, such as schools and universities, medical clinics(诊所) and hospitals, recreational facilities and sports stadiums, retail chain stores and large shopping centers, warehouses and light manufacturing plants, and skyscrapers for offices and hotels. The owners of such buildings may or may not be familiar with construction industry practices, but they usually are able to select competent professional consultants and arrange the financing of the constructed facilities themselves. Speciality architects and engineers are often engaged for designing a specific type of building, while the builders or general contractors undertaking such projects may also be specialized in only that type of building.

Specialized industrial construction Specialized industrial construction usually involves very large scale projects with a high degree of technological complexity, such as an oil refineries, steel mills, chemical processing plants are deeply involved in the development of a project, and prefer to work with designers-builders so that the total time for the completion of the project can be shortened. They also want to pick（选择）a team of designers and builders with whom the owner has developed good working relations over the years.

Infrastructure（地下结构）and heavy construction Infrastructure and heavy construction include projects such as highways, mass transit systems, tunnels, bridges, pipelines, drainage（排水）systems and sewage plants（污水处理厂）, Most of these projects are publicly owned and therefore financed either through bonds（债券）or taxes（税收）. This category of construction is characterized by a high degree of mechanization, which has gradually replaced some labor intensive operations.

Reading material Ⅱ

Lhasa, Capital of Tibet & the Highest city in the World

The City of Lhasa（拉萨）has always presented a strong fascination（魅力）to people both within and outside Tibet. Every year, thousands of Tibetans come to Lhasa to pay homage to their holy city. Foreign friends from different countries would like to fly to the city for a visit for its mysterious（神秘的）temples.

Lhasa, the world's highest city, is in fact a small city with a population of 150,000. Yet, the many ancient temples arouse much of the visitors' interest. They are attracted by Norpu Garden, the Dazhao Temple, famous for its architectural beauty, the Drepon Temple, the third biggest temple in the world. What strikes them most, however, is the Potala Palace（布达拉宫）.

In the seventh century, the well-known Tibetan King Songzan Ganbu had the palace built under the suggestion of Princess Wencheng. A thousand years later, the palace was rebuilt. And that was the Potala Palace we see today. With a height of 110 meters, the Palace stands on the top of the Red

Mountain, covering an area of about 130,000 square meters. Valuables of various kinds are kept in there.

Since the "Peaceful Liberation" in 1950, Tibet has been dotted with modern buildings, highways, power stations, and suspension bridges. Lhasa is making headway. The present Lhasa is a combination of the old and new. Lhasa is beautiful, and so are its people.

It was on July 1, 2006 that China opened a new railway called the Qinghai-Tibet railway with the first passenger train leaving for Tibet from Qinghai Province.

Lesson 10 Cost Estimation of Construction Project

Text

Cost estimation is one of the most important steps in project management. Cost estimation establishes the base line of the project cost at different stages of development of the project. A cost estimate at a given stage of project development represents a prediction provided by the cost engineer or estimator on the basis of available data. Due to different agencies, construction cost estimate can adopt different point of view. Although project cost estimation used in different stages have many types, but according to its function, cost estimates can be divided into three categories. Construction cost estimate provides one of the following three basic functions: investment estimation, design budgetary estimate and construction drawing budget[1].

Investment Estimation

Investment estimation is to point to in the process of project investment decision-making, on the basis of the existing data and the specific method, estimates the amount of investment of construction project. In project proposal, pre - feasibility study, feasibility study, project design phase (including concept design and approval scheme design) investment estimation should be compiled[2].

1. The role of investment estimation

Investment estimation of the project proposal stage is one of the basis of project examination and approval by the competent department of project proposal, and plays a role of reference for project planning and scale.

The investment estimation of project feasibility study stage, is the important basis of project investment decision.

Project investment estimation controls engineering design estimation, design budgetary estimate shall not break through the approved amount of investment, and should be controlled within the amount of investment estimate;

Project investment estimation can be used as the basis of project financing and construction loan plan, the construction unit according to the approved project investment estimates, can finance and to apply for a loan from the bank.

The project investment estimation is the important basis of the calculation of the investment of fixed assets in the construction projects and the preparation of the investment plan of fixed assets.

2. The basic steps of construction project investment estimation

(1) Respectively to estimate the project construction cost required by each single items of projects as a project, equipment and instruments purchase expense, installation cost.

(2) On the basis of summary the cost of each unit project to estimate the engineering construction fees and other basic reserve funds.

(3) Estimate the spread of reserve funds

(4) Estimate interest incurred during construction

(5) Estimate the liquidity

(6) Summary the total investment

Design budget estimation

Design budgetary estimate is a rough calculation of construction project investment quota at the design stage, design budget estimate of investment should include the construction project from the project, feasibility study, design, construction, commissioning to completion inspection and acceptance of all the construction funds, budget is an important part of the design documents, the approval design documents, must be approval design budgetary estimate of the file at the same time. Adopt two stages design of construction projects, design budget estimation must be prepare in the preliminary design stage; adopt the three stage design, the revised estimation must be prepared in expand preliminary design stage. The control, approval, and adjustment of design budget quota should follow the relevant provisions of the state, local governments of provinces and cities, or industry. If the design budgetary estimate of value is more than controlled budgetary that because of budget quota changes affect the economic benefits of the project. Economic benefits are not up to a predetermined revenue goals, the project design must be modified or re-approval again.

1. The role of the design budget estimation

(1) Budget is the base of fixing asset investment plan, determine and control investment of construction project.

The state stipulates that formulate annual plan of investment in fixed assets, and determine the amount of total investment planned and its components must be on the basis of the preliminary design estimation. Without approval of preliminary design documents and estimation, construction project would not be included in the annual fixed asset investment.

(2) Design budgetary estimate is the base of signing contract for construction project contracting and loan contract.

Explicitly stipulated in the contract law issued by the state, contract price of the construction project is based on design estimation, budget price, and the investment total contract shall not exceed the investment of the design general estimate. Bank loans or cumulative total of appropriations must not exceed the design budgetary estimate, if the project investment plan is listed by investment and loan breakthrough design budgetary estimate, the reason must be found out, then, the construction unit reported to higher authorities adjustment or additional design estimates a total investment, before ratified, the bank refused to allocate part of its cost overruns.

(3) Design budgetary estimate is the base of controlling construction design and construction drawing budget.

Design unit must design construction drawing in accordance with the approved preliminary design and general estimate, construction drawing budget cannot break through the design budget estimates, if really need to break through the general estimate, the project should be in accordance with the prescribed procedures and approval[3].

(4) Design estimate is base of measuring the rationality on economic and technology of design and choosing the best solutions.

In preliminary design stage design department choose the best design, design budgetary estimate is the important basis of measuring economic rationality of design scheme from the economic angle. Design budgetary estimate, therefore, is the base of measuring the rationality on economic technology of design, and choosing the best solutions.

(5) Budget is the basis of assessing effect for construction project investment

Through the comparison of design estimates and final accounts, we can analyze and assess that investment results is good or bad, while verifying the accuracy of estimate, and it is helpful to strengthening the design management and cost management of construction project budget estimate.

2. The method of design estimate

Design budgetary estimate can be divided into three levels: estimate for unit project, comprehensive estimate for single items of projects and total estimate for construction projects.

Building total budget of the project is to determine the entire construction project from planning to completion and acceptance of all the required documents, it is formed by the estimates of single items of projects as a comprehensive other expenses, engineering construction, the construction period of reserve funds, loan interest and the investment direction regulating tax budgetary estimate of total staff.

Comprehensive estimates of individual projects are comprehensive documents to determine individual project construction costs, it is up to the individual engineering project budget which must be gathered, and it is integral part of construction project budget estimates.

Unit engineering budgetary estimate is to determine the project construction cost files, is the basis of comprehensive estimates of individual projects, and also is a part of the comprehensive budget of individual projects.

Construction drawing budget

Construction figure budget is that units engineering budget book, it happens after construction figure design completed and before engineering starts. according to the approved construction drawings, under the construction scheme and construction organization design have been identified, according to the consumption quota, the billing rules and the budget of man, machine, material prices, to compile economic documents about the project cost determined.

The basis of compiling construction drawing budget includes construction drawings, construction organization and design documents, engineering budget quota, estimate for the price list or unit, artificial wage budget price, materials, the unit price of construction machinery affecting, budget engineering manuals, project contracting contract documents[4].

Construction drawing budget establishment has two methods: unit price method and physical method.

1) The unit price method

The unit price method is to use a good estimate which has been compiled for the units of the sectional works to prepare the construction drawing budget. According to construction drawing to calculate all kinds of construction quantities, and multiplied by the corresponding unit price, gather together, get unit engineering of the sum of labor, materials, machinery fee; and plus program calculated in accordance with provisions of other direct fees, the funds, indirect fees, planned profits and taxes, can be concluded that the unit project construction drawing budget cost. This method is advantageous for the technical and economic analysis, and is one of the commonly used preparation methods.

2) Physical method

Physical method is firstly according to the construction drawings to calculate the sub - project volumes respectively, and then form the corresponding budget labor, materials, mechanical machine - team norm dosage, then respectively multiplied by the project located at the time of labor, materials, machinery, seeking out units engineering of artificial fee, and material fee and construction mechanical using fee, and summary sum, then obtaine directly engineering fee, last by provides meter take other the costs, last summary on can obtained units engineering construction figure budget cost.

New Words and Phrases

1. investment estimation　[ɪnˈvestmənt ˌestɪˈmeɪʃn]　投资估算
2. budget　[ˈbʌdʒɪt]　预算
3. feasibility study　[ˌfiːzəˈbɪlətɪ ˈstʌdi]　可行性研究
4. finance　[ˌfaɪnæns]　资金筹措
5. asset　[ˈæset]　资产
6. equipment　[ɪˈkwɪpmənt]　设备，装备
7. purchase　[ˈpɜːtʃəs]　购买；采购
8. installation cost　[ˌɪnstəˈleɪʃn kɔst]　安装工程费
9. reserve funds　[rɪˈzɜːv fʌndz]　预备费
10. investment quota　[ɪnˈvestmənt ˈkwəʊtə]　投资额度
11. preliminary design estimation　[prɪˈlɪmɪnəri dɪˈzaɪn ˌestɪˈmeɪʃn]　初步设计概算
12. final account　[ˈfaɪnəl əˈkaʊnt]　竣工决算

Notes

[1] Although project cost estimation used in different stages have many types, but according to its function, cost estimates can be divided into three categories. Construction cost estimate provides one of the following three basic functions: investment estimation, design budgetary estimate and construction drawing budget.

由于不同的机构要求，建筑成本估算可采用不同的观点。尽管项目不同阶段使用的成本估算有很多类型，但根据其功能不同，成本估算可划分为三大类。建筑成本估算提供以下三种基本功能之一：投资估算、设计概算和施工图预算。

[2] In project proposal, pre-feasibility study, feasibility study, project design phase (including concept design scheme design and approval) investment estimation should be compiled.

在项目建议书、预可行性研究、可行性研究、方案设计阶段（包括概念方案设计和报批方案设计）应编制投资估算。

[3] Design unit must design construction drawing in accordance with the approved preliminary design and general estimate, construction drawing

budget cannot break through the design budget estimates, if really need to break through the general estimate, the project should be in accordance with the prescribed procedures and approval.

设计单位必须按照批准的初步设计和总概算进行施工图设计,施工图预算不得突破设计概算,如确需突破总概算时,应按规定程序报批。

[4] The basis of compiling construction drawing budget includes construction drawings, construction organization and design documents, engineering budget quota, estimate for the price list or unit, artificial wage budget price, materials, the unit price of construction machinery affecting, budget engineering manuals, project contracting contract documents.

施工图预算的编制的依据包括施工图纸、施工组织设计文件、工程预算定额、价目表或单位估价表、人工工资标准、材料预算价格、施工机械台班单价、预算工程手册、工程承发包合同文件。

参 考 译 文

第 10 课 建筑工程造价估算

造价估算在项目管理过程中是最为重要的步骤之一。它建立了项目发展不同阶段项目成本的底线。在项目发展的不同阶段所做出的成本估算体现了造价工程师或预算员以可利用资料为基础所做的预测。由于不同的机构要求,建筑成本估算可采用不同的观点。尽管项目不同阶段使用的成本估算有很多类型,但根据其功能不同,成本估算可划分为三大类。建筑成本估算提供以下三种基本功能之一:投资估算、设计概算和施工图预算。

投资估算

投资估算是指在项目投资决策过程中,依据现有的资料和特定的方法,对建设项目的投资数额进行的估计。在项目建议书、预可行性研究、可行性研究、方案设计阶段(包括概念方案设计和报批方案设计)应编制投资估算。

1. 投资估算的作用

项目建议书阶段的投资估算,是项目主管部门审批项目建议书的依据之一,并对项目的规划、规模起参考作用。

项目可行性研究阶段的投资估算,是项目投资决策的重要依据。

项目投资估算对工程设计概算起控制作用,设计概算不得突破批准的投资额,并应控制在投资估算额以内。

项目投资估算可作为项目资金筹措及制定建设贷款计划的依据,建设单位可根据批准的项目投资估算额,进行资金筹措和向银行申请贷款。

项目投资估算是核算建设项目固定资产投资需要额和编制固定资产投资计划的重要依据。

2. 建设项目投资估算的基本步骤

(1) 分别估算各单项工程所需的建筑工程费、设备及工器具购置费、安装工程费。

(2) 在汇总各单项工程费用的基础上,估算工程建设其他费用和基本预备费。

(3) 估算价差预备费。

(4) 估算建设期利息。

(5) 估算流动资金。

(6) 汇总出总投资。

设计概算

设计概算是在设计阶段对建设项目投资额度的概略计算,设计概算投资包括建设项目从立项、可行性研究、设计、施工、试运行到竣工验收等的全部建设资金,设计概算是设计文件的重要组成部分,在报批设计文件时,必须同时报批设计概算文件。采用两阶段设计的建设项目,初步设计阶段必须编制设计概算;采用三阶段设计的,扩大初步设计阶段必须编制修正概算。设计概算额度控制、审批、调整应遵循国家、各省市地方政府或行业有关规定。如果设计概算值超过控制额,以至于因概算投资额度变化影响项目的经济效益,使经济效益达不到预定收益目标值时,必须修改设计或重新立项审批。

1. 设计概算的作用

(1) 设计概算是编制固定资产投资计划,确定和控制建设项目投资的依据。

国家规定,编制年度固定资产投资计划,确定计划投资总额及其构成数额,要以批准的初步设计概算为依据,没有批准的初步设计文件及其概算,建设工程就不能列入年度固定资产投资计划。

(2) 设计概算是签订建设工程承发包合同和贷款合同的依据。

在国家颁布的合同法中明确规定,建设工程合同价款是以设计概、预算价为依据,且总承包合同不得超过设计总概算的投资额。银行贷款或各单项工程的拨款累计总额不能超过设计概算,如果项目投资计划所列支投资额与贷款突破设计概算时,必须查明原因,之后由建设单位报请上级主管部门调整或追加设计概算总投资,未批准之前,银行对其超支部分拒不拨付。

(3) 设计概算是控制施工图设计和施工图预算的依据。

设计单位必须按照批准的初步设计和总概算进行施工图设计,施工图预算不得突破设计概算,如确需突破总概算时,应按规定程序报批。

(4) 设计概算是衡量设计方案技术经济合理性和选择最佳设计方案的依据。

设计部门在初步设计阶段要选择最佳设计方案,设计概算是从经济角度衡量设计方案经济合理性的重要依据。因此,设计概算是衡量设计方案技术经济合理性和选择最佳设计方案的依据。

(5) 设计概算是考核建设项目投资效果的依据。

通过设计概算与竣工决算对比，可以分析和考核投资效果的好坏，同时还可以验证设计概算的准确性，有利于加强设计概算管理和建设项目的造价管理工作。

2. 设计概算的方法

设计概算可分为单位工程概算、单项工程综合概算和建设项目总概算三级。

建设项目总概算是确定整个建设项目从筹建到竣工验收时所需全部费用的文件，它是由各单项工程综合概算、工程建设其他费用概算、预备费、建设期贷款利息和投资方向调节税概算汇总编制而成的。

单项工程综合概算是确定单项工程建设费用的综合性文件，它是由该单项工程的各专业的单位工程概算汇总而成的，是建设项目总概算的组成部分。

单位工程概算是确定各单位工程建设费用的文件，是编制单项工程综合概算的依据，也是单项工程综合概算的组成部分。

施工图预算

施工图预算即单位工程预算书，是在施工图设计完成后，工程开工前，根据已批准的施工图纸，在施工方案或施工组织设计已确定的前提下，根据消耗量定额，计费规则及人、机、材的预算价格编制的确定工程造价的经济文件。

施工图预算的编制依据包括施工图纸、施工组织设计文件、工程预算定额、价目表或单位估价表、人工工资标准、材料预算价格、施工机械台班单价、预算工程手册、工程承发包合同文件。

施工图预算的编制方法有单价法和实物法两种。

1）单价法

单价法是用事先编制好的分项工程的单位估价表来编制施工图预算的方法。按施工图计算的各分项工程的工程量，并乘以相应单价，汇总相加，得到单位工程的人工费、材料费、机械使用费之和；再加上按规定程序计算出来的其他直接费、现场经费、间接费、计划利润和税金，便可得出单位工程的施工图预算造价。这种编制方法便于技术经济分析，是常用的一种编制方法。

2）实物法

实物法是首先根据施工图纸分别计算出分项工程量，然后套用相应预算人工、材料、机械台班的定额用量，再分别乘以工程所在地当时的人工、材料、机械台班的实际单价，求出单位工程的人工费、材料费和施工机械使用费，并汇总求和，进而求得直接工程费，最后按规定计取其他各项费用，最后汇总就可得出单位工程施工图预算造价。

Reading material Ⅰ

Estimate, Bidding and Costs

Particular attention should be given to the answers to the question: For whom is the estimate being prepared and for what purpose? The answers will influence the contractor as to the amount of time and effort that should be expended on preparation of the estimate, and also indicate how serious the organization should be about attempting to negotiate a contract at the figure submitted. Decision on the latter should be made at an early date, even before the estimate is prepared, so that the type of estimate can be decided.

Bid Documents

The Documents should be examined for completeness of plans and specifications, and for the probable accuracy that an estimate will yield from the information being furnished. For example, sometimes contract documents are sent out for bid when they are only partly complete and the owner does not seriously intend to award a contract at that stage but merely wishes to ascertain whether construction cost will be acceptable.

Preparation of the Top Sheet

This is usually based on an examination of the specifications table of contents. If there are no specifications, then the contractor should use as a guide top sheet from previous estimate for jobs of a similar nature, or checklists.

Subcontractor Prices

Decide on which trades sub-bids will be obtained, and solicit prices from subcontractors and suppliers in those trades. These requests for prices should be made by postcard, telephone or personal visit.

Decide on which trades work will be done by the contractor's own forces, and prepare a detailed estimate of labor and materials for those trades.

Pricing

Use either unit prices arrived at from the contractor's own past records, estimates made by the members of the contractor's organization, or various reference books that list typical unit prices spreadsheets of unit price for various types of work on different structures may be maintained by a contractor. These can be updated electronically with new wage and material costs, depending on the program used, so that prices can be applied nearly automatically.

Hidden Costs

Carefully examine the general conditions of the contract and visit the site, so as to have a full knowledge of all the possible hidden costs, such as special insurance requirements, portions of site not yet available, and complicated logistics.

Final Steps

Receive prices for materials and subcontracts. Review the estimate and carefully note exclusions and exceptions in each subcontracts bid and in material quotations. Fill in with allowance or budgets those items or trades for which no price are available.

Decide on the markup. This is an evaluation that should be made by the contractors, weighting factors such as the amount of extras that may be expected the reputation of the owner, the need for work on the general contractor and the contractor's overhead.

Finally, and most importantly, the estimate must be submitted in the form requested by the owner. The form must be filled in completely, without any qualifying language or exceptions, and must be submitted at the time and place specified in the invitation to bid.

Reading material II

The Eiffel Tower, a Symbol of Paris

The Eiffel Tower in Paris needs no presentation. It is one of the most well-known monuments in the world visited by more than 5 million people each year.

Built in May 1889 for the Universal Exhibition in celebration (庆祝) of the French Revolution, the tower is located on the southern bank of the Seine River (塞纳河).

The magnificent Eiffel Tower has become the symbol of Paris ever since it was set up. The Tower is more than 300 meters high and consists of an iron frame work supported on four masonry piers, from which rise four columns uniting to form one shaft (轴). Three platforms at different heights are reached by stairs and elevators. On top of the Tower are a meteorological (气象的) station, a wireless station, and a television transmission antenna.

Designed by the famous French engineer with the name of Eiffel, the whole project was completed in twenty-one and a half months and cost 7,799,401 francs.

Lesson 11　Green Building

Text

What is a green building?　Green Building refers to in building life cycle, the maximum conservation of resources (energy, land, water and material), protecting the environment and reducing pollution, providing people with healthy, appropriate and efficient use of space, and nature harmony of the building. The so-called green building "green" does not mean general sense of three-dimensional green, roof garden, but represents a concept or symbol, refers to building environmentally and friendly, makes full use of natural resources, but also known as a sustainable building, eco-building, back into the wild construction, energy saving construction.

Green building interior layout is very reasonable, to minimize the use of synthetic materials, full use of the sun, saves energy for the residents and creates almost-natural feeling.

People, architectures and the natural environment for the harmonious development goals, in the use of natural and artificial means to create good conditions and healthy living environment, as much as possible to control and reduce the use and destruction of the natural environment, to fully reflect the nature obtain and balance.

Building energy saving, initially refers to reduce the loss of energy in buildings, but now commonly known as "improving energy efficiency in the building", that is, people can rationally use energy and constantly improve energy use efficiency, under the premise of improve the comfort of buildings. It is to define the scope of building energy use, including air-conditioning, heating, lighting, household appliances, cooking, and other aspects of energy consumption.

Sustainable Design　Sustainability represents a balance that accommodates human needs without diminishing the sound development and productivity of natural systems[1]. The American Institute of Architects defines sustainability as "the ability of society to continue functioning into the future of the key resources on which that system depends", In these times of rapidly rising world population, increased demand on scarce resources, and continued pollution, sustainability is quickly becoming the dominant issue of our time. It is an issue that each of us, individually and as institutional representatives, can and should address in our daily work.

Different climatic regions of the impact of energy-saving　Geographical feature of the climate zones in China have great influence on the design of energy efficient building, shown in Fig 11.1. In accordance with the climatic conditions in China, is divided into five zones: severe cold, cold, hot summer/cold winter, hot summer/warm winter, and temperate.

Fig11.1 Different climate zones in China

In severe cold and cold regions, building energy-saving design develop relatively early and it has been more experience, the main consideration is the winter insulation. In hot summer and cold winter areas, it can be said that the greatest potential in energy saving. Design should considerate the insulation balance in summer and winter. Generally in hot summer and warm winter areas, the main consideration is the summer insulation. In temperate areas, more attention should be paid to the summer insulation and little attention be paid to the winter insulation.

Energy saving measures Ideal green buildings should demand following points in least energy consumption, one is in different season and different areas that can control reception and prevent sun radiation. Secondly, it can keep the comfort of room in different seasons. Thirdly, necessary ventilation and gas exchange can be realized. At present, the methods of building energy conservation mainly include: trying to reduce consumption of non-reproductive energy, improving using efficiency of energy, reducing energy loss of building enclosure structure, decreasing the energy loss of building establishment operation. In these three sides, high techniques play a crucial role. Of course, building energy conservation also adopts some traditional techniques, but it is based on advanced experiment reasoning and scientific theory analysis.

1. Reducing Energy Consumption and Improving On Efficiency of Energy Usage

In order to retain environment quality of living space, warmness is required in cold season to improve temperature of room; cold is required in hot season to reduce temperature of room, both of them usually need consume energy to realize them. From the angle of energy conservation, the efficiency of heating or refrigeration should be improved. It includes the efficiency of equipment itself, efficiency of tube net transfer, measure of user end and the efficiency of control equipment of room inside environment. These all require high and new techniques in design, setting, run quality, energy conservation system modulation, equipment materials and management model industries. At present, there are three types of new techniques in the aspect of heating system energy conservation. (a) Tube net flux is distributed reasonably through using computer, balance valve and aptitude meter. It not only perfects heating quality, but alsos save energy. (b) Quantity of heat assign meter and thermoregulation valve are set in user radiator. (c) New types of heat preservation materials package tubes are used to reduce heat loss of tube.

2. Reducing Energy Loss of Building Envelop

The external envelop of the construction is one of the important parts of the building heating loss positions: within whole the heating loss, the external wall seizes 25%~28%, the roof 7%~8%, doors & windows radiation 25%~28%, and the permeation of doors & windows 23%~28%. High efficient building envelop could improve the effect of heat preservation and insulation, as well as reducing the required energy during the process of the operation.

1) Energy conservation techniques of external wall

As far as wall energy conservation is concerned, the traditional method is that applying heavy single material to increase wall thickness to attain heat preservation. Composite wall body usually is comprised with RC and heat insulation materials. At present, the production of materials of building requires particular craftwork and equipment, rather than traditional techniques.

(1) External wall heat preservation and decoration face system.

The system occurred in the last energy crisis in the end of last century seventy ages, firstly used in the commercial building, then applied in the civil buildings. Today, EIFS system (Exterior Insulation and Finish System) takes account of 17.0% in the utilization of external wall of commercial building, 3.5% in the civil buildings, and it grows rapidly at the rate of 17%-18% every year in the using of civil buildings[2]. This system is external wall heat preservation with much layer heat preservation, applied in the civil and commercial buildings. ELFS system includes the following three parts: the main part is heat preservation board made of polystyrene foam plastic, it is commonly 1~4 inch thick, fixed to building outer wall in the fashion of synthetic plastering agent or mechanism. Long and waterproof polymer slurry grass-roots in the middle part, which mainly used on the heat preservation board and transmit outside force in fiberglass net. Beautiful and long surface covered layer is outside part, shown in Fig 11.2.

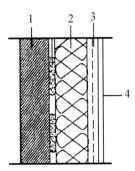

Fig11.2 EIFS System
1—exteral wall; 2—preservation board;
3—Warter proof polymer slurry grass-roots; 4—surface

(2) Building heat preservation and insulation board system.

This system can be used as wall body and floor board in the civil and commercial buildings. In the middle of the board material is polystyrene plastic with filling layer, it is commonly 4—8 inch thick, different board face layer can be adopted in two surfaces according to requirement[3]. The buildings of this material have the characteristic of high strength, good effect of heat preservation, low price, simple construction, energy conservation and environmental protection. SIPS (Structural Insulated Panels) has commonly a width of 4 inch, and at most it can come to a length of 24 inch. The size has been a series, and many plants can make it according to engineering need and practical size, and can be supplied in the form of whole set, and truly realize industrialization of house production.

(3) External wall system of heat insulation and cement mould.

This product is one type of insulation and mould system, made from polystyrene foam plastic. When construction, it is level or upright and matched with steel bar, after wall body is constructed, the insulation mould will be a part of permanent wall body, then concrete wall body of heat preservation and insulation can be formed inside and outside wall body at the same time. The mould material outside concrete wall surface meets the requirement of heat preservation, noise isolation and fireproofing.

2) Energy conservation techniques of door and window

Doors and windows have the roles of lighting, ventilation and enclosure structure, and it plays an important role in the art treat. But door and window are parts that caused easily energy loss. In order to increase lighting and ventilation areas, the doors and windows areas of buildings becomes bigger, there will be veil wall buildings of all glass. This provides higher requirement to outer enclosure structure energy conservation. At present, the treat with energy conservation of door and window mainly perfects heat preservation performance and improves close performance. In our country, after twenty century ninety ages, plastic door and window are used greatly, and will replace steel and aluminum materials with high energy loss. In order to solve problems that caused great energy loss by big area glass, people apply high techniques to process common glass to various particular glasses.

3) Energy conservation techniques of roof

Heat preservation and insulation are very important in enclosure structures energy conservation. In cold areas, heat preservation layer should be set up to prevent the loss of room heat. In hot areas, it can prevent solar radiation heat to transfer to inside of room. But in the winter cold and summer hot areas, building energy conservation should consider winter heat preservation and summer insulation. The common technique for heat preservation is to set light material with little heat transfer coefficient to preserve energy. The methods of heat insulation and temperature decrease list as follows: built on stilt floors to ventilate, store water in roof, spray water in time and green roof. These methods all demand the requirement of energy conservation in roof to different extent. But the most popular is the utilization of aptitude techniques and ecology techniques.

3. Exploiting and Utilization of New Energy

For saving non-renewable energy sources, man still look for and exploit and utilize new energy to adjust to the reality that population increase and energy decrease. This task is endowed with modern people by history, and the exploiting and utilization of new energy are certain to depend on high technology. For example, when we exploit and utilize solar energy, wind energy, tide energy, water power, terrestrial heat and other renewable natural energy, we must resort to advanced technique methods, and perfect and improve it to utilize energy more, people can utilize solar efficiently. For example energy to heating, solar energy water heater can transfer solar energy to electricity energy.

New Words and Phrases

1. green building   [gri:n ˈbɪldɪŋ]   绿色建筑
2. sustainable design   [səˈsteɪnəbl dɪˈzaɪn]   可持续设计

3. resource	[rɪˈsɔːs]	资源
4. commodity	[kəˈmɒdəti]	商品
5. household appliances	[ˈhaʊshəʊld əpˈlaɪənsɪz]	家用电器
6. efficiency	[ɪˈfɪʃnsi]	效率
7. energy-saving	[ˈenədʒiːˈseɪvɪŋ]	节能
8. ventilation	[ˌventɪˈleɪʃn]	通风、换气
9. insulation	[ˌɪnsjuˈleɪʃn]	绝热，保温，隔热
10. environment	[ɪnˈvaɪrənmənt]	环境
11. enclosure	[ɪnˈkləʊʒə(r)]	围护结构，围隔
12. polystyrene foam plastic	[ˌpɒliˈstaɪriːn fəʊm ˈplæstɪk]	聚苯乙烯泡沫塑料
13. craft work	[krɑːft wɜːk]	工艺
14. veil wall	[veɪl wɔːl]	幕墙
15. stilt floor	[stɪlt flɔː]	架空层
16. exploit	[ɪkˈsplɔɪt]	开发
17. endow	[ɪnˈdaʊ]	赋予
18. conservation	[ˌkɒnsəˈveɪʃn]	保护，节约

Notes

[1] Sustainability represents a balance that accommodates human needs without diminishing the sound development and productivity of natural systems.

可持续代表的是一种在不减弱自然系统的健康发展和生产能力的基础上便能够满足人类需求的一种平衡。

[2] Today, EIFS system (Exterior Insulation and Finish System) takes account of 17.0% in the utilization of external wall of commercial building, 3.5% in the civil buildings, and it grows rapidly at the rate of 17%～18% every year in the using of civil buildings.

今天，外墙外保温系统占到了整个商业建筑外墙保温的17%，民用建筑的3.5%，并且在民用建筑中的使用率以每年17%～18%的增长率增加。

[3] In the middle of the board material is polystyrene plastic with filling layer, it is commonly 4～8 inch thick, different board face layer can be adopted in two surfaces according to requirement.

在板中间的材料是带有填充层的聚苯乙烯塑料，通常有4～8英寸厚，要根据在两个板面上的工程要求，采用不同的板层厚度。

参考译文

第11课 绿色建筑

什么是绿色建筑？绿色建筑是指在建筑物的生命周期，最大限度地节约资源（节能、节地、节水、节材），保护环境和减少污染，为人们提供健康、舒适和高效的使用空间，与建筑自然和谐相处。所谓绿色建筑的"绿色"，并不意味着一般意义上的全面绿化、屋顶花园，而是体现一种概念或象征，指建筑环境良好，充分利用自然资源，也称为一个可持续建筑、生态建筑、自然建筑、节能建筑。

绿色建筑的室内布局十分合理，尽量减少使用合成材料，充分利用自然采光，为居民节约能源，并创建几乎自然的感觉。

人，建筑与自然环境的和谐发展的目标，是在利用天然和人工手段来创造良好和健康的生活环境的同时，尽可能地控制和减少对自然环境的使用和破坏，充分反映自然获取和平衡。

建筑节能，最初是指减少建筑物中能量的流失，现在则普遍称为"提高建筑物中的能源利用率"，即在保证提高建筑物舒适度的前提下，人们能够合理使用能源并不断提高能源利用效率。它所界定的范围是指建筑使用能耗，包括空调、采暖、照明、家用电器、炊事等方面的能耗。

可持续设计 可持续代表的是一种在不减弱自然系统的健康发展和生产能力的基础上便能够满足人类需求的一种平衡。美国建筑师学会将可持续定义为"将这个系统赖以运转的重要资源持续不断地运用至将来的一种社会能力"。在世界人口激增、稀有能源需求增加、持续污染的年代中，可持续正迅速成为当今世界发展的主题。这是我们每一个人，作为个体也好、作为机构的代表也好，在日常工作当中都应当重视的一个问题。

不同气候地区对建筑节能的影响 在中国，气候区的地理特点对建筑节能设计有很大的影响，如图11.1。针对中国的气候条件，划分了5个地区：严寒、寒冷、夏热冬冷、夏热冬暖和温暖地区。

在严寒和寒冷地区，

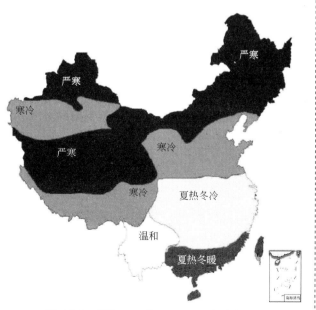

Fig11.1　Different climate zones in China

建筑节能的设计相对起步较早，经验比较丰富，主要考虑的是冬季保温。在夏热冬冷地区，可以说是最有潜力的节省能源地区。设计应该考虑冬季和夏季隔热的平衡。一般在夏热冬暖地区，主要的考虑是夏季保温。在暖和地区，更多地是考虑夏季隔热，而较少关注冬季保温。

理想的绿色建筑至少在能源消耗方面应满足下面几点的要求，一是在不同的季节和不同的地区能够控制接收和防止太阳辐射；其次，在不同的季节它能够保持室内的舒适；第三，必要的通风和气体交换能够得以实现。目前，建筑节能方法主要包括：尽量减少非可再生能源的消耗，提高能源使用效率，减少建筑围护结构的能源损耗，降低建设过程中的能量损失。在这三个方面，高技术发挥了至关重要的作用。当然，建筑节能也采取了一些传统技术，但它是基于先进的实验推理和科学的理论分析。

1. 减少能源消耗和改善能源使用的效率

为了保持生活空间的环境质量，在寒冷季节，需要用供热来改善房间的温度；在高温季节，需要用制冷来降低房间的温度，这些通常都需要消耗能源来实现它们。从节约能源角度来看，加热或制冷的效率应予改善，它包括设备本身的效率，管网转换的效率，终端用户的使用方法和室内环境的控制设备的效率。这些在设计，设置，运行质量，能源节约系统的调制，设备材料和行业的管理模式上都需要高新技术。目前，在供热系统节约能源方面有三种类型的新技术：（a）通过使用计算机，使管网流量分布合理，它不仅完善了供热质量，而且还节省能源；（b）在用户的散热器上设置热度计量表和温度调节阀；（c）使用新型的保温材料包裹管道，以减少管子的热损失。

2. 减少建筑物围护结构的能耗

外围护结构是建筑热量损失的重要部位：整座建筑热散失中，外墙占25%～28%，屋面占7%～8%，门窗散热占25%～28%，门窗渗透占23%～28%。高质量的建筑外围护结构能够有效地提高建筑的保温隔热效果，减少建筑在运行过程中所需的能耗。

1) 外墙节能技术

就墙体节能而言，传统的方法是使用重型的单一材料来增加墙厚以获得保温。复合墙体通常是由钢筋混凝土和绝热材料组成。目前，建筑材料的生产需要特别的工艺和设备，由传统技术是不能完成的。

（1）外墙外保温和装饰面系统。

这种系统出现在20世纪70年代的能源危机时期，首先在商业建筑中，然后在民用建筑中采用。今天，外墙外保温系统占到了整个商业建筑外墙保温的17%，民用建筑的3.5%，并且在民用建筑中的使用率以每年17%～18%的增长率增加。这是由很多绝热层组成的外墙外保温系统，应用在民用和商业建筑中。外墙外保温系统包括以下三个部分：主要部分是由聚苯乙烯塑料构成的保温板，通常它有1～4英寸厚，用人工合成或机制的石膏剂固定在外墙上。长期的、防水的聚合物水泥浆基层在系统的中间，主要是用在保温板上来传递玻璃纤维网承受的外部荷载。美观长久的装饰面层在系统的最外面，如图 11.2 所示。

(2) 建筑保温隔热墙板系统。

这个系统可以用作民用和公共建筑中的墙体和地板。在板中间的材料是带有填充层的聚苯乙烯塑料，通常有 4～8 英寸厚，要根据在两个板面上的工程要求，采用不同的板层厚度。这种材料的建筑物具有强度高、保温效果良好、价格低廉、施工简单、节能和环保的特点。SIPS（结构绝热墙板）通常有 4 英寸宽，并且至多能达到 24 英寸长。由于尺寸范围广，取材方便，成套供应，使得这种墙板真正实现了建造房屋的工业化。

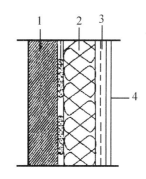

图 11.2　外墙外保温系统
1—外墙；2—保护层；
3—防水层；4—面层

(3) 外墙水泥模板保温系统。

这种产品是一种绝热模板系统，由聚苯乙烯泡沫塑料制成。在施工中，它可以是水平或者竖直的，并和钢筋配合，墙体施工完毕之后，保温模板将成为墙体永久的部分，因此混凝土墙体内侧和外侧的保温隔热将同时形成。在混凝土墙外侧的模板材料满足了保温、隔声和防火的要求。

2）门窗节能技术

门窗承担采光、通风和围护的作用，并在建筑艺术上发挥了重要作用，但门窗是很容易造成能量损失的部分。为了增加通风及照明的地方，建筑物的门窗变得更大，有的建筑物是全部玻璃的玻璃幕墙，这对外部围护结构的节能提出了更高的要求。目前，门窗节能的处理方法，主要是完善保温性能，同时增强密闭的效果。在我国，20 世纪 90 的年代之后，塑料门窗的使用增多，它将取代高能量损失的钢和铝材。为了解决由使用大面积玻璃幕墙而造成的极大的能量损失的问题，人们应用高科技将普通玻璃改进为各种特种玻璃。

3）屋顶节能技术

保温隔热在围护结构节能方面非常重要。在寒冷地区，应设置保温层以防止室内的热损失。在炎热地区，隔热层可以防止太阳辐射的热量传到室内。但在夏热冬冷地区，建筑节能应考虑冬季的保温和夏季的隔热。常见的保温技术是使用传热系数很小的轻质材料来维护能源。隔热和温度下降的方法如下：建造架空层来通风，在屋面蓄水，在屋顶及时洒水和种植。这些方法在屋顶建筑节能上有不同的需要范围。但最流行的是利用智能技术和生态技术。

3. 开发利用新能源

为了节约非可再生能源，人们一直在寻找和开发利用新能源来适应人口增长和能源减少的现实。这项任务是历史赋予现代人们的，并且开发利用新能源一定会依赖于高科技。举例来说，当我们开发利用太阳能、风能、潮汐能源、水利电力、地热和其他可再生自然能源时，我们必须诉诸于先进的技术方法，并通过健全和完善它以利用更多能源，人们可以高效地利用太阳能。例如用来采暖，太阳能热水器可以使太阳能转换成电能。

Reading material Ⅰ

High-rise building energy-saving

Along with the reform and opening-up and the rapid development of economy, China's high-rise buildings built in a high-rise building, In high-rise building toward a higher, more strong direction at the same time, the energy saving design the general trend of development in human body to improve and health and improving the conditions of comfort, energy efficiency, rational utilization of resources, reduce greenhouse gas emissions, protecting environment for human survival. Therefore, high-rise building energy saving has become the world's architectural community, the concern of Chinese construction has become a hot issue.

High-rise building in shanghai

1. High-rise building energy saving in the application situation

High-rise building efficiency is a complicated system engineering, from high-rise building ontology technology to high-level building materials products, high-rise building with equipment of thermal environment there are energy saving potential. Therefore, high-rise building energy saving should be in guarantee its use function, construction quality and the premise of indoor environment, and adopts various effective energy saving technology and management measures.

2. High-rise building energy saving development prospects

In China the high-rise buildings from energy-saving work in the early 1990s just start. Therefore, we should do: first, energy aspect in design technology, actively adopt energy-saving building materials, new energy-saving wall body, the roof insulation technology, energy-saving door window insulation and airtight technology, increasing new and renewable energy such as solar energy and low thermal can in high-rise buildings, and further promote the application of different energy heat pump technology, products and recycling waste heat, waste heat technology; Secondly, in the high-rise building energy-saving design management, to strengthen high-level building energy efficiency standardization work, strictly enforce the energy-saving design of high-rise building, high-rise building energy-saving design as high-rise building design meets the standards important assessment project; Again, in the high-rise building, the use of equipment products should adopt the energy-saving heating and air-conditioning equipment, and improve the energy efficiency of equipment operation, in order to achieve the purpose of energy-saving better.

Reading material Ⅱ

The White House, the Presidential Mansion of the U. S. A

Construction of the "Presidential Mansion" began in 1792. Still unfinished, drafty and uncomfortable, it was first occupied by John Adams and his family in 1800. Mrs. Adams made most of her new home and hung the wash in the East Room.

The British burned the White House in the War of 1812. President James Madison (詹姆斯·麦迪逊总统) fled, but his wife Dolley Madison saved the famous Gilbert Stuart portrait of Washington.

The White House is located in the heart of the capital and is surrounded by beautiful park-like gardens. During the American Civil War, troops (军队) protecting Washington were bivouacked (露宿) on the lawn, and military quarters were set up in the East Room. During World War I there were no troops stationed there, but sheep gazed on the White House grass.

During President Harry Truman's administration in 1948, the White House was discovered to be on the verge of collapse (倒塌). Massive rebuilding and renovation were required, but the original floor plan was reserved. During her husband's administration, Mrs. John F. Kennedy tried to restore the interiors as it was in the early eighteen hundreds.

Lesson 12　Profile: Liang Ssu-ch'eng

Text

Liang Ssu-ch'eng (April 20, 1901—January 9, 1972)(Fig 12.1) was the son of Liang Qichao, a well-known Chinese thinker in the late Qing Dynasty. By inheritance and training Liang was superbly fitted to the role fate assigned him-leader of the first generation of Chinese architectural historians[1]. Knowledge of China's great traditions and its forward movements was deeply inculcated in the son. Liang was slight of stature and by nature observant, curious, careful, and aesthetically sensitive. He loved to draw and was talented musically. Though he had been born in Tokyo where his father was a temporary political refugee, he grew up in Beijing. There he received his initial preparation in the two educational spheres that would prove vital for his future achievements. These were, first, the traditional training supervised by his father in classical Chinese that he would need for studying old books, and second, a firm grounding in English language, Western sciences, and humanities at Tsing Hua College, specifically designed to prepare students for further study abroad[2].

Fig 12.1　Liang Ssu-ch'eng (1901—1972)

Chance played its part in Liang's choice of architecture as a career. It was suggested by the girl who was later to become his wife, Lin Whei-yin (known in the United States as Phyllis Lin). From a British schoolmate who played at designing houses, she learned of the profession of architect. Attracted to a lifework that combined daily artistic creativity with immediate usefulness, she decided this was the profession she wanted. On her return to China she easily won Liang to the same decision.

Both Liang and Lin Whei-yin (Fig 12.2) decided to study at the University of Pennsylvania Department of Architecture headed by the eminent Paul Cret from Paris. Liang's entry was delayed until the fall term of 1924 by a disastrous motorcycle accident in Beijing in May 1923 that caused multiple fractures of his left leg. It never healed properly and remained slightly shorter than his right leg. Lin Whei-yin also reached Penn in the fall term of 1924, only to discover that women were not admitted to the Department of Architecture. She enrolled in the university's School of Fine Arts.

Fig 12.2　Liang Ssu-ch'eng and Lin Whei-yin

During the second year of Liang at Penn, he received from his father in Beijing a book that was destined to affect his entire life. It was a key to Sung dynasty architecture, the Ying-tsao fa-shih, compiled in 1103 by a brilliant official at the Sung court, which set forth in unfamiliar terminology the techniques of Sung construction. It had essentially disappeared in succeeding centuries but a manuscript copy had recently been discovered and published. Liang tackled the book at once, but he admitted later that he understood very little. Beforehand he had apparently given little thought to Chinese architectural history, but from now on the challenge to solve the obscurities of this key works was fixed in the back of his mind.

The wedding of Liang and Lin Whei-yin, deferred at his father's urging until both had completed their studies, took place in March 1928 in Ottawa. After wedding the young couple experienced the grand tour of Europe by car, hunting out the monuments they had studied. It was the first of the many architectural field trips they were to share in the years to come.

After they returned to China, Liang was appointed in September 1928 to establish and head a Department of Architecture at Northeastern University in Shenyang. In 1931, three years after Liang had joined the university faculty, when a Japanese military coup seized control of the northeastern provinces, they moved back to Beijing.

This autumn of blighted hopes marked a decisive turn in Liang's career. He had accepted in June a new position, which led to his most productive years as an architectural historian. The Society for Research in Chinese Architecture had been established in Beijing in 1929 by Chu Ch'I-ch'ien, as a consequence of his discovery of the Ying-tsao fa-shih.

The Society's headquarters were rooms just inside the Tian An Men on the west side of the courtyard. There, in the autumn of 1932 Liang resumed his earlier study of the Sung manual. It seemed so promising, yet most of the technical terms still eluded him. His practical training and experience told him, as he expressed it, that "the only reliable sources of information are the buildings themselves and the only available teachers are the craftsmen". He conceived the idea of starting his research by studying the construction of the palace buildings around him under the tutelage of certain old carpenters who had spent their lives maintaining them[3]. Most of buildings had been erected in the Qing dynasty (1644—1912). A Qing handbook of structural regulations, the Kung-ch'eng tso-fa tse-li, had been published in 1734. It was filled with equally unfamiliar technical terms, but the old crafts men knew orally the traditional terms, and with their guidance Liang was able to identify the various timbers and other structural parts, to observe the complex building methods, and to decipher the regulations cited in the manual[4]. This firsthand research resulted in his first book, Qing-tai ying-taso tse-li (Qing Structural Regulations), which discussed and explained the Qing manual[4].

In this way, Liang achieved his first insight into what he called "the grammar of Chinese architecture". He was still puzzled and challenged by the Ying-tsao fa-shih, with its data about eleventh-century buildings. But experience had convinced him that the key was to find and examine surviving building of that period. The time had come for wide-ranging field trips. Then Liang and his wife began a program of field trips, prepared by careful searching in the kind of literature that could be counted on to cite and locate local monuments, the county or provincial gazetteers, most of which carried back at least to the 18th century[5].

Several of these trips were notably successful, and their results were published in the society's quarterly. Liang's first field trip, made in 1932, resulted in one of his greatest discoveries. It was the towering Buddhist structure, Tu-le Ssu, located sixty miles east of Beijing, which housed a clay figure fifty-five feet high. Both the wood-frame building, erected in 984 AD, and the statue had survived over a thousand years in good condition. The high point of their years of searching was the discovery in June 1937 of a Buddhist temple, Fo-kuang Ssu, built in 857 AD. This beautiful structure, located deeply in the mountains of northern Shansi province, had endured in good condition for over a thousand years and was recognized by Liang to be the oldest wooden building yet discovered in China and the first one of Tang Dynasty.

He and his family, with some members of the Society, had left Beijing in the summer of 1937 as the city was falling to the Japanese. They made their way in the great refugee migration to the mountain-ringed southwestern provinces, which were still controlled by the Chinese government. There the

Society was made an Institute of the National Academy, Academic Chinese, with Liang in charge. Surveys of the architecture of Yunnan and Szechuan were undertaken. But as the eight years of war, isolation, and soaring inflation continued, illness and poverty worsened, many members of the group left for their own life. Liang remained in Li-chuang with his family, his faithful assistant, Mo Tsung-chiang, and a few others. Lin Whei-yin was confined to bed with tuberculosis. It was in such circumstances that Liang, in 1946, with his wife's help as always, composed this, his only book written in English, to acquaint the outside world with the achievement of the Institute for Research in Chinese Architecture during the previous fifteen years[6].

After the war, Liang was appointed to establish the architectural and planning programs at Tsinghua University. In 1946, he stayed at Princeton University as a visiting fellow and served as the Chinese representative in the design of the United Nation Headquarters Building. In 1947, Liang received an honorary doctoral degree from Princeton University. This time, Alarm and grief at the crisis in his wife's precarious health were enough to distract Liang.

In 1949 the newly established People's Republic of China turned to Liang for counsel and leadership in rebuilding, city planning, and other architectural matters. Even the gravely ill Lin Whei-yin participated in designing at the request of the government before her early death in 1955.

During the Cultural Revolution, Liang Ssu-ch'eng was condemned as "an authority of counter-revolutionary scholarship" and suffered severe persecution. He died in Beijing in 1972, four years before the Cultural Revolution ended. He was subsequently rehabilitated.

New Words and Phrases

1. heritance   [ˈherɪtəns]   遗传，遗产
2. inculcate   [ˈɪnkʌlkeɪt]   谆谆劝导
3. observant   [əbˈzɜːvənt]   深切注意的
4. aesthetically   [esˈθetɪklɪ]   审美地，美学观点上地
5. talented   [ˈtæləntɪd]   有才能的
6. refugee   [ˌrefjʊˈdʒiː]   难民，流亡者
7. supervised   [ˈsuːpəvaizd]   监督，管理，指导
8. immediate   [ɪˈmiːdiət]   直接的，紧接的，紧靠的，立即的，知觉的
9. eminent   [ˈemɪnənt]   显赫的，杰出的，有名的，优良的
10. disastrous   [dɪˈzɑːstrəs]   损失惨重的，悲伤的
11. fracture   [ˈfræktʃə(r)]   破裂，骨折

12. brilliant	[ˈbrɪliənt]	灿烂的，闪耀的，有才气的
13. setforth	[set fɔːθ]	阐明，宣布，提出，陈列，出发，把（会议等）提前
14. terminology	[ˌtɜːmɪˈnɒlədʒi]	术语学
15. manuscript	[ˈmænjʊskrɪpt]	手稿，原稿
16. obscurity	[əbˈskjʊərəti]	阴暗，朦胧，偏僻，含糊，隐匿，晦涩，身份低微
17. deferred	[dɪˈfɜːd]	延期的，缓召的
18. grand tour	[grænd tʊə]	从前英国贵族子女的遍游欧洲大陆的教育旅行（上流社会子女作为毕业的最后一部分）
19. faculty	[ˈfæklti]	全体教员
20. craft	[krɑːft]	工艺，手艺
21. conceived	[kənˈsiːvd]	构思，以为，持有，怀孕，考虑，设想
22. carpenter	[ˈkɑːpəntə]	木匠
23. erect	[ɪˈrekt]	盖，使竖立，使直立，树立，建立
24. field trip	[fiːld trɪp]	实地考察旅行
25. gazetteer	[ˌgæzɪˈtɪə]	地名辞典，记者，公报记者
26. Buddhist	[ˈbʊdɪst]	佛教的
27. migration	[maɪˈgreɪʃn]	移民，移植，移住，移动
28. tuberculosis	[tjuːˌbɜːkjʊˈləʊsɪs]	肺结核
29. honorary	[ˈɒnərəri]	荣誉的，名誉的
30. persecution	[ˌpɜːsɪˈkjuːʃn]	迫害，烦扰
31. rehabilitat	[ˌriːəˈbɪlɪteɪt]	使（身体）康复，使复职，使恢复名誉，使复原

Notes

[1] By inheritance and training Liang was superbly fitted to the role fate assigned him-leader of the first generation of Chinese architectural historians.

天赋及后天培养使梁思成可以出色完成命运赋予他的重任——成为中国第一代建筑师学家的领导者。

[2] These were, first, the traditional training supervised by his father in classical Chinese that he would need for studying old books, and second, a firm grounding in English language, Western sciences, and humanities at Tsing Hua University, specifically designed to prepare students for further study abroad.

一方面是在其父亲的监督下在清华学堂学习中国古典文学，这为他奠定了良好的中文基础；另一方面是学习英语，西方自然科学及西方人文科学，而这为他出国深造做好了充分的准备。这一阶段的学习对他今后事业的成功起到了至关重要的作用。

[3] He conceived the idea of starting his research by studying the construction of the palace buildings around him under the tutelage of certain old carpenters who had spent their lives maintaining them.

怀着这样的想法,他找到长期维修宫廷建筑的木匠师傅,开始对他周围的宫廷建筑的结构进行研究。

[4] It was filled with equally unfamiliar technical terms, but the old crafts men knew orally the traditional terms, and with their guidance Liang was able to identify the various timbers and other structural parts, to observe the complex building methods, and to decipher the regulations cited in the manual.

《工程做法则例》中有大量不熟悉的术语,但是那些老工匠们能口述这些术语,在他们的帮助下梁思成可以辨认大量的木构件及其他构件,得知这些复杂建筑的建造方法,并对书中的规则术语进行解释。

[5] Then Liang and his wife began a program of field trips, prepared for by careful searching in the kind of literature that could be counted on to cite and locate local monuments, the county or provincial gazetteers, most of which carried back at least to the 18th century.

梁思成和他的妻子开始了他们的实地考察计划:搜集省、县级地方志中所记载的当地的名胜古迹,这些地方志大部分都可以将历史追溯到18世纪。

[6] It was in such circumstances that Liang, in 1946, with his wife's help as always, composed this, his only book written in English, to acquaint the outside world with the achievement of the Institute for Research in Chinese Architecture during the previous fifteen years.

在这样的情况下,1946年梁思成在妻子一如既往的帮助下将研究所过去15年对中国建筑所做的调查展示给外界,并完成了他唯一一本用英语编写的书。

参 考 译 文

第12课 梁思成简介

梁思成(1901.4.20—1972.1.9)(图12.1)是中国晚清著名政治家梁启超之子。天赋及后天培养使梁思成可以出色完成命运赋予他的重任——成为中国第一代建筑师学家的领导者。中国传统的知识和先进的思想哺育着华夏儿女,也赋予清瘦的梁思成稳重、谨慎、好奇的性格和对美学特有的敏感,而且他喜欢绘画,并在音乐方面很有天赋。梁思成出生于日本东京(当时他的父亲在此政治避难),在北京长大。在清华学堂,他接受到来自两个领域的教育:一方面是在其父亲的监督下学习中国古典文学,这为他奠定了良好的中文基础；另一方面是学习英语、西方自然科学及西方人文科学，而这为他出国深造做好了充分的准备。这一阶段的学习对他今后事业的成功起到了至关重要的作用。

与一个女孩的邂逅使得梁思成选择建筑学作为自己的职业。这个女孩就是他后来的妻子林徽因（美国名字 Phyllis Lin）。她从英国一位从事房屋设计的同学那里了解到建筑学专业，认为这个专业可以将艺术和现实紧密地结合在一起，值得用一生去学习。在林徽因回国期间，梁思成受到她的影响也做出了同样的选择。

图 12.1　梁思成（1901—1972）

梁思成和林徽因（图 12.2）决定去美国宾夕法尼亚大学建筑系学习，师从来自巴黎著名的 Paul Cret。由于 1923 年 5 月在北京的一场车祸致使得梁思成左腿多处骨折，因此他直到 1924 年秋季才到达学校。这次骨折并没被彻底治愈，以至于后来其左腿稍跛。林徽因也是在 1924 年的秋季到达宾夕法尼亚大学，然而却发现学校不允许女孩子学习建筑。于是她选择就读于该大学的美术学院。

图 12.2　梁思成和林徽因

在宾夕法尼亚大学的第二年，梁思成收到了一本父亲寄自北京的、影响其一生的书。这是一本关于宋朝建筑的书籍——《营造法式》，由宋朝一名官员于 1103 年完成，阐述了宋代的结构技术术语。这些术语在宋朝随后的年代原已基本消失，此时手抄本又被重新发现，并予以出版。得到该书后，梁思成马上对其进行研究，但理解甚少。之前他很少留意中国古建筑史，但是从那时起他就下定决心来研究这本晦涩难懂的书。

在父亲的催促下，梁思成和林徽因在双方均完成各自的学业后，于 1928 年 3 月在渥太华完婚。婚后他们乘车开始了毕业前的欧洲之旅，游览书本上学过的名胜古迹。这是他们人生中第一次共同实地考察。

回国后，1928年9月梁思成在沈阳大学创立建筑系并被任命为系主任。1931年，即梁思成担任系主任的第三年，日本占领东北，他们举家搬回北京。

这个秋季是梁思成的人生转折点。他在1931年6月接受了一个新的职务，此后的几年开创了他作为一名建筑学大师在事业上的多产期。营造学社是朱启钤在发现《营造法式》后，于1929年在北京成立的，目的是对中国建筑进行研究。

营造学社的总部设在天安门西侧庭院的几间房子里。1931年秋季梁思成再次对他曾经研读过的宋朝手册进行研究。起初他对此很有信心，然而后来他发现还是有很多的术语难以理解。经验告诉他："真正可靠的来源是建筑物本身，唯一能寻求到的老师是工匠师傅。"怀着这样的想法，他找到长期维修宫廷建筑的木匠师傅，开始对他周围的宫廷建筑的结构进行研究，其中大部分的建筑建于清朝（1644—1912）。1734年清工部印制的清朝结构章程手册——《工程做法则例》中有大量不熟悉的术语，但是那些老工匠们能口述这些术语，在他们的帮助下梁思成可以辨认大量的木构件及其他构件，得知这些复杂建筑的建造方法，并对书中的规则术语进行解释。《清式营造算例及则例》便是他第一手的研究成果，书中讨论并解释了清代那本手册。

梁思成以这样的方式完成了他谓之"中国建筑法则"的第一次洞察。但是他对《营造法式》中描述的11世纪的建筑还是感到迷惑。但是经验使他确信寻找和考察现存的宋代建筑才是解决问题的关键。于是大范围的实地考察工作开始了。梁思成和他的妻子开始了他们的实地考察计划：搜集省、县级地方志中所记载的当地的名胜古迹，这些地方志大部分都可以将历史追溯到18世纪。

其中几次实地考察特别成功，他们将考察结果发表在营造学社期刊上（还是季刊）。1932年梁思成的第一次实地考察便是他几次最伟大的考察之一。佛教杰出的建筑——独乐寺，位于北京东60km处，寺内一尊高55英尺的泥塑佛像以及木构建筑，皆是建于公元984年，距今已有一千多年了，仍然保存完好。他最伟大的发现是在1937年对佛光寺的考察。这座美丽的建筑建于公元857年，位于山西省五台山，历经千年沧桑至今完好无损。梁思成认为这个建筑是国内年代最久远的唐代建筑。

1937年日本占领北京，当年夏天梁思成携家人及营造学社的一些成员离开北京。他们开始了向由中国政府控制的西南部深山地区逃亡。在此成立了国家科学院研究所，由梁思成负责，对四川、云南的建筑进行考察。由于八年战争、通货膨胀的延续、疾病、经济的困扰，许多成员为生计所迫离开研究所。梁思成和他的忠诚助手莫宗江以及少数的研究所成员则继续留在李庄。而林徽因因肺结核卧床不起。在这样的情况下，1946年梁思成在妻子一如既往的帮助下将研究所过去15年对中国建筑所做的调查展示给外界，并完成了他唯一一本用英语编写的书。

战争结束后，梁思成被任命去清华大学建立建筑及规划方案项目。1946年他去普林斯顿大学做访问学者，被任命为纽约联合国总部大厦设计咨询委员会的中国代表，1947年获普林斯顿大学名誉博士学位。此时妻子病情的日益严重,这让梁思成感到无比痛苦和担心,使他没有足够的精力顾及其他。

1949年新中国委任梁思成领导关于城市规划、重建及其他建筑事务的工作。林徽因即便重病卧床也应政府之邀参加设计工作,直到1955年去世。

梁思成在文革期间被冠以"反动学术权威"遭到严重迫害,于1972年在北京逝世(此时距"文化大革命"结束还有4年)。后来对其进行平反并恢复名誉。

Reading material Ⅰ

Olympic Buildings in Beijing

In the build up to the Olympics city officials hired some of the world's leading architects, and if you're looking for a conversation here in Beijing just mention some of the new buildings that have sprung up.

The Night View of the National Stadium

1. Beijing National Stadium——Bird's Nest

The Beijing National Stadium, also known as the National Stadium, or colloquially (用通俗语) as the "Bird's Nest" for its architecture, is a stadium in the Olympic Games in Beijing. The venue hosted the opening and closing ceremonies of the Beijing Olympic Games and Paralympics Games (残奥会), the track and field competitions, and the football finals. Its design, specifications and construction are there.

Design, Specifications

Pritzker Prize-winning architects Herzog & de Meuron, Arup Sport and China Architecture Design & Research Group designed this building. The ground was broken on December 24, 2003, construction started in March 2004, and it was completed in March 2008.

The stadium had a seating capacity of 91000 during the Olympic

Games. The capacity has reduced to 80000 now. The stadium cost up to 3.5 billion yuan, 110000 tons of steel were used in the Stadium, making the stadium the largest steel structure in the world, and 42 thousand tons of steel beams woven (编织) together in the shape of bird's nest.

The main body of the National Stadium has a design life of 100 years. Its fire resistance capability is first-rate, and it can withstand an eight-magnitude earthquake. The water-resistance capability of its underground project is also first-rate. The main body of the National Stadium is a colossal saddle-shaped elliptic (椭圆马鞍形) steel structure. It is 333 meters long from north to south, 294 meters wide from east to west, and 69 meters tall. The stadium uses 258000 square meters of space and has a usable area of 204000 square meters.

Construction and material

The main body's elements support each other and converge into a grid formation, just like a bird's nest with interlocking (连接的) branches and twigs (小枝). Being a seven-story shear wall system, the stadium's stand has a concrete framework.

The upper part of the stand and the stadium's steel structure are separated from each other, but both are based on a joint footing. The roof of the National Stadium is covered by a double-layer membrane structure, with a transparent (透明的) ETFE (聚氟乙烯) membrane (膜), fixed on the upper part of the roofing structure and a translucent PTFE membrane fixed on its lower part. A PTFE (聚四氟乙烯) acoustic (声学的) ceiling is attached to the side walls of the inner ring. The high tech membrane lets in sunlight to conserve energy, keeps the noise in, rain and wind out.

The construction team branded a kind of new steel for the bird's nest, called Q460, never before used in China. This product was 110mm thick plate steel, surpassing the previous national standard of 100mm for this type of steel. The new domestically produced steel can withstand earthquakes, low temperatures and is suitable for welding.

Significance

Now, the stadium becomes a large-scale sports and entertainment facility for the residents of Beijing - an architectural landmark and Olympic legacy (遗产).

2. National Aquatics Center-Water Cube

National aquatics center

The Beijing National Aquatics Center, the landmark building of Beijing 2008 Olympic Games, also known as the National Aquatics Center, better known as the Water Cube is an aquatics center that was built alongside Beijing

The Nightscape of the "Water Cube"

National Stadium in the Olympic Green for the 2008 Summer Olympics. Ground was broken on December 24, 2003, and the Center was completed and delivered for use on January 28, 2008. Despite its nickname（昵称）, the building is a cuboid（立方体的）(rectangular box), not a cube.

The National Aquatics Center's construction area is close to 80000 square meters, containing 17000 standard seats, including 6000 permanent seats and 11000 temporary ones which was removed after the Olympic games. The Aquatics Center has hosted the swimming, diving and synchronized swimming events during the Olympics.

The achievement of Olympics

Many people believe Water Cube to be the fastest Olympic pool in the world. It is 1 meter deeper than most Olympic pools. Deeper pools allow the waves to dissipate down to the bottom, leading to less water disturbance to the swimmers. The pool also has perforated gutters（凿孔的槽）on both sides to absorb the waves. With the popularity of the newly introduced faster Speedo LZR Racer（一种名牌泳衣）swim suit, the Aquatics Center saw 23 world records broken in the Beijing Olympics.

Design

The Water Cube was designed by a consortium made up of PTW Architects (an Australian architecture firm), Arup international engineering group, CSCEC (China State Construction Engineering Corporation), and CCDI (China Construction Design International) of Shenzhen.

The Water Cube's design was initiated by a team effort, and the Chinese partners felt a square was more symbolic to Chinese culture and its relationship to the bird's nest stadium, while the Australian partners came through with the idea of covering the "cube" with bubbles, symbolizing water.

Architecture

The membrane structure of the "Water Cube", which is composed of more than 3000 pneumatic die cushions (气枕) with a coverage area of 110000 square meters, is the largest in the world. The "Water Cube" is also the only public building that is fully made of a membrane structure. The ETFE membrane has good ductility (展延性) and crushing resistance (抗碾性). After aeration (通风), every piece of membrane can resist the weight of a car. It also has good resistance against fire and intense heat.

The "Water Cube" can breathe: Eight fans which discharge the air naturally are set on the roof and the body of the "Water Cube". After fresh air enters the building, it can be discharged through the cavum (空腔) in the roof. This is how the heating within the building is released.

The "Water Cube" can "wash its face" by itself: The ETFE membrane is self-cleaning in nature. Since the friction coefficient (摩擦系数) of the material is small, dust does not easily attach onto the structure. Even if dust does collect on it, as long as it rains, the surface is washed by rain water.

The "Water Cube" was built in accordance with a water-saving design concept to be a gigantic (巨大的) green architectural wonder.

The venue's membrane structure is not only the first of its kind in China and the world's largest and most complex ETFE project, but it is also an economical and water-saving creation.

The blue-colored "hubble-bubble" material is much lighter than conventional glazing structures with the same lighting effect. So the cost of its supporting steel structure was reduced considerably.

In addition, the "Water Cube" was designed with water-saving and environmental protection efforts. According to statistics, the outer surface and roof facade can "collect" 10000 tons of rain water, 70000 tons of clean water and 60000 tons of swimming pool water annually. And the venue can also save 140000 tons of recycled water a year.

The water cube has set a new standard in environmental sports design, not only in China but aslo throughout the world.

Reading material II

Hong Kong, Known as the "Pearl of the East"

Hong Kong is part of China, which lies to the south of Guangdong Province. It is made up of three parts: Hong Kong Island, Kowloon and New Territories. Hong Kong has an area of more than 1,000 square kilometers. There are about 6,000,000 people living there. It has not only the modern seaport but also the famous Qide International Airport. The newly-built railway from Beijing to Kowloon connects Hong Kong with the capital of our country. Hong Kong is known as the "Pearl of the East". It is one of the largest trade centers in the world. Its scenery (风景) is so beautiful and the climate is so pleasant that travelers throughout the world come to visit it.

People there are mainly Chinese. The Chinese people play a very important part in building New Hong Kong. The people of Hong Kong are fond of peace. Since the policy of "One nation, two systems", Hong Kong keeps in close touch with the mainland. The relationship between the two sides is getting better and better. That Hong Kong was returned to China and became one of China's special administrative regions on July 1st, 1997 stands for the wish of the Chinese people, including the people of Hong Kong.

Lesson 13 Building Information Modeling (BIM)

Traditional ways of working are insufficient to meet the unrelenting need for new and rehabilitated infrastructure amid today's economic realities. The methods by which projects are delivered and assets are managed must undergo a fundamental change in order to meet critical objectives. Improved productivity and transparency will help to close the gap between soaring investment demand and limited access to capital.

Building Information Modeling (BIM) is the vehicle by which the business of planning, designing, building, and managing the world's infrastructure will be transformed to deliver higher productivity, quality, and cost-effectiveness.

The use of BIM gives this often diverse group of stakeholders a shared understanding of the project through a model-centric approach which keeps them connected to a more accurate and up-to-date view. [1] Miscommunication, design errors, and, in turn, risk are mitigated while decision making is improved with the ability to use the model to simulate nearly all aspects of the project.

The entire process of developing, executing and managing infrastructure projects can be transformed - initial surveying and data collection, environmental review, public participation, design and documentation, bidding, construction, operations and maintenance. The model-centric approach enables planners, engineers, and designers to explore and validate innovative design ideas and what-if scenarios with project investors. Before ground is broken, all parties have a better understanding of scheduling (4D) and cost (5D), environmental impacts are assessed and understood, and the public can visualize what the project will look like at various stages of completion[2].

With BIM, project information is available and actionable throughout every phase of the infrastructure lifecycle. The whole project team was able to view the construction model, using the same up-to-date information when assessing how best to perform construction tasks. The ability to use information-rich models to track and visualize progress even facilitated the budgeting and payment process.

Planning

Every infrastructure project begins with existing conditions, and massive

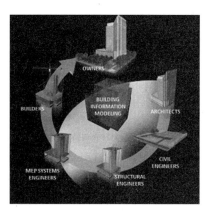

Fig. 13.1　The process of Building Information Modeling from the designer to the owner

amounts of data. And for owner organizations, the ability to simultaneously analyze scheduling and costs for multiple projects across a major capital program is hugely valuable. Right away, a BIM approach can improve the accuracy and speed of the planning process by helping to aggregate multiple types of data from a variety of sources into a single reference model.

This comprehensive view of existing conditions provides all stakeholders with greater clarity—which can help inform their decisions. Visualizations from this information-rich model can be shared with non-professional stakeholders, helping to ease approvals and further speed the planning process.[3] Just as important, the information and decisions at this point are captured in the model and will remain consistent through project completion.

Preliminary design

Using the existing conditions model, designers can then work with 3D concepts in a representation of the actual environment. Using BIM helped the team to confidently select this unusual alternative because the process was able to simulate real-word performance and help the public envision how it would look and function once completed.

Detailed design

The complexity of many infrastructure projects requires intense multidisciplinary collaboration. Since the model is comprised of data-rich objects with defined relationships to each other and to the environment, immensely useful information is accessible by all project stakeholders, who in turn can contribute to the model—all without loss of data fidelity.

Construction and program management

Without the data continuity and discipline coordination that the BIM process enables, information is lost and must be recreated at every hand-over. By contrast, BIM conserves and uses information across the lifecycle of an infrastructure asset.

Historically, at the end of the design stage a construction firm received 2D plan sets that often dumbed down much of the engineering data that went into creating those plans. These flat document sets then became the primary interface between builders and designers and owners. This not only inhibits collaboration, increases risk, and works against design fidelity, it can create onerous rework for contractors on competitive bid projects.

Owner organizations are plagued with issues deriving from poor communication. BIM systematically dismantles that problem by providing owners greater program control, ultimately enhancing major capital program construction planning. [4]

Using the BIM process, the design model is available earlier to better inform preconstruction planning for activities such as staging, sequencing, scheduling, quantity take-off, and estimating. Given access to the model, contractors can produce more accurate bids in less time by evaluating various coordination activities, such as temporary roads, location of material, and other logistics prior to breaking ground. Construction operations are also facilitated by the BIM process, as data can be added to the model to support schedule (4D) and cost (5D) project management.

The operations and maintenance phase of the infrastructure asset will persist longer than any other project phase, so advantages gained here have cumulative effects. Using a BIM process operators have access to the richest information streams ever created, including detailed data from the post-construction model and information from real-time sensors that continuously update the model during operation.

Asset management, operations and maintenance

That owners and operators can benefit from rich, detailed information about a particular asset is intuitively obvious, however, owner/operators are usually responsible for a wide array of interconnected and often interdependent assets. BIM facilitates improved management and analysis of project-level information, which can be used in large-scale integrated asset management workflows.

Modern model-based design applications, which use visualization tools that were developed for the gaming industry, provide an environment that is much more familiar and stimulating for the millennial generation than 2D CAD drawings. Cloud computing and collaboration platforms make the process of planning and designing infrastructure more intuitive, social, and immediate.

New Words and Phrases

1. accurate ['ækjərət] 精确的
2. budget ['bʌdʒɪt] 预算

3.	cumulative	[ˈkjuːmjələtɪv]	累积的
4.	facilitate	[fəˈsɪlɪteɪt]	使便利；推进
5.	fidelity	[fɪˈdeləti]	逼真；保真度
6.	gap	[gæp]	缺口
7.	infrastructure	[ˈɪnfrəstrʌktʃə]	基础设施；基础建设
8.	intuitively	[ɪnˈtjuːɪtɪvli]	直觉地，直观地
9.	lifecycle	[ˈlaɪfsaɪkl]	生命周期
10.	mitigate	[ˈmɪtɪgeɪt]	减轻，缓和
11.	multidisciplinary	[ˌmʌltɪdɪsəˈplɪnəri]	多学科的
12.	participation	[pɑːˌtɪsɪˈpeɪʃn]	参加
13.	scenarios	[sɪˈnɑːriəʊz]	情景
14.	sequencing	[ˈsiːkwənsɪŋ]	先后顺序；定序
15.	soaring	[ˈsɔːrɪŋ]	猛增的
16.	unrelenting	[ˌʌnrɪˈlentɪŋ]	无情的；冷酷的
17.	validate	[ˈvælɪdeɪt]	使合法化；使生效；批准

Notes

[1] The use of BIM gives this often diverse group of stakeholders a shared understanding of the project through a model-centric approach which keeps them connected to a more accurate and up-to-date view.

BIM 以模型为基础，通过 BIM 的使用，有助于不同的参与方对项目达成共识，能让各方看到准确、及时更新的信息模型。

[2] Before ground is broken, all parties have a better understanding of scheduling (4D) and cost (5D), environmental impacts are assessed and understood, and the public can visualize what the project will look like at various stages of completion.

破土动工前，各项目参与方已了解项目施工进度计划（4D）、项目成本控制（5D），并对环境影响进行了解和评估。公众可以看到项目任意阶段完成后将呈现的效果。

[3] Visualizations from this information-rich model can be shared with non-professional stakeholders, helping to ease approvals and further speed the planning process.

该模型信息丰富，且具有可视性，有利于非专业的项目相关方更容易理解，从而加快规划进程。

[4] BIM systematically dismantles that problem by providing owners greater program control, ultimately enhancing major capital program construction planning.

BIM 为业主提供了系统的解决方法，能让业主更好地控制项目，最终改善重大投资项目的建设规划。

参考译文

第13课 建筑信息模型（BIM）

在当今的经济形势下，传统方式不足以应对人们对新建基础设施及重建基础设施的日益增长的需求。关键目标的实现要求必须改变项目交付方式和资产管理方式。提高工作效率，增加透明度，有助于缩小飙升的投资需求和有限的资金之间的差距。

作为全球基础设施规划、设计、建设和管理的方式，BIM（建筑信息模型）带来了更高的生产效率、质量和成本效益。

BIM以模型为基础，通过BIM的使用，有助于不同的参与方对项目达成共识，能让各方看到准确、及时更新的信息模型。信息模型几乎能模拟项目的所有环节，在此基础上做出的决策会更好，能降低因沟通不畅、设计错误带来的风险。

基建项目的开发、执行和管理过程都将被改变，涉及初步测量和数据采集、环境评审、公众参与、设计和文件编制、投标、施工、运营和维护。这种以模型为中心的方法使规划师、工程师和设计师能与项目投资者共同探索和验证新的设计理念和不同的设计方案。破土动工前，各个项目参与方都对项目施工进度计划（4D）、项目成本控制（5D）和项目对环境影响有了很好的了解，可以看到项目任意阶段完成后将呈现的效果。

BIM的使用有利于随时收集、及时处理与基建项目整个生命周期内各个阶段的相关信息。整个项目团队能都通过建筑模型，利用最新共享的信息模型，寻求项目建设的最佳方法。模型能提供大量信息，使项目具有可追踪性和可视化，有利于预算和支付完成。

Fig 13.1 BIM在项目整个过程中的应用

规划

每一个基建项目开始时都涉及对现场数据的收集及地貌情况。业主能同时分析重大投资计划中多个项目的调度和成本的能力显得至关重要。恰恰

BIM能把多种来源的数据整合成一个模型，从而提高规划方案的质量和速度。

对现存情况的全面了解能让所有参与方更清晰地了解投资计划，做出更好的决策。该模型信息丰富，且具有可视性，有利于非专业的项目相关方更容易理解，从而加快规划进程。此阶段的决策会在信息模型中体现，这些信息会与项目的实施保持一致。

初步设计

利用当前信息模型，设计人员可以用3D模拟实际情况。项目团队对BIM很信任的原因是因为它能模拟真实情况，能可视化竣工后的情况。

细节设计

很多基建项目极其复杂，需要多学科协作。因为BIM模型信息丰富，并且明确规定了各方之间以及各方与环境之间的关系，所以所有工程参与方都能接触到有价值的信息，并且利用所得信息去完善BIM模型，同时保证了数据的真实性。

施工管理

没有BIM数据的连续性和多学科协作，每次交接都会出现信息丢失和重复工作的现象，而BIM可以保存并利用项目整个生命周期中所有的信息。

以前，在设计的最后阶段，建筑公司收到2D设计图，这些图纸过度简化了很多指导施工的数据。作为建设者、设计师和业主之间的主要接口，这些平面图纸不仅严重影响了各方的协作，增加了风险，降低了设计作品的保真度，而且还会对承包商的竞标项目造成严重的返工。

业主面临着沟通不畅引发的诸多问题。BIM为业主提供了系统的解决方法，能让业主更好地控制项目，最终改善重大投资项目的建设规划。

BIM的使用有利于更快完成设计模型，可以更有效地通知各方施工前的规划活动，如工期、工序、进度、工程量统计、估算。利用该模型评估各种活动（如临时道路、材料的位置和其他动工前的准备情况），使承包商的投标会更快、更精确。由于数据可以被添加到模型中支持项目管理的进度（4D）和成本（5D），BIM也有利于施工作业的顺利进行。

基础设施资产运营与维护阶段比其他阶段都长，所以，该阶段的优势有积累效应。采用BIM，营运人员能接触到有史以来最丰富的信息流，包括竣工后的模型的详细数据和施工过程中实时传感器不断传送的模型的更新信息。

运营维护

资产所有者和运营者从丰富、详细的信息中得到的帮助是显而易见的，但是他们经常要负责大量的、常常相互关联、相互依存的资产，而BIM有利于改善可用在大型综合资产管理工作中的信息的管理和分析。

以模型为基础的现代设计应用程序，采用了游戏产业开发的可视化工具，模拟出了更逼真的环境，比起二维的CAD图纸，更具有颠覆性。云计算和协作平台让基础设施规划和设计过程更直观、更社会化、更即时。

Reading material Ⅰ

Planning a House

Building a house is an operation (施工) which costs quite a lot of money. Suppose you plan to build a house. Your first step will be to find a suitable piece of land. Your choice will depend on various things. You will probably try to find a sunny place, in a pleasant situation, near stores and bus stops, not too far from your friends and the place where you work.

Next you will find an experienced builder. The builder will work out drawings according to your request. There are three kinds of drawings: elevations (立面图), planes (平面图) and sections (剖面图).

An elevation is the view of one side of a building. A building with four sides has four elevations. Elevations show the shapes and sizes of the outside doors and windows. They show their positions (位置) in the walls.

A plane is the view of a building from above. It shows the thickness (厚度) of the outside wall and the inside wall, and the positions of the doors and windows. You need several planes for your house. For a small, one-storey house, for example, you need a foundation (基础) plane, a first floor plane and a roof plane.

A section cuts the house from top to bottom. It shows the height of the rooms inside the building and the thickness of the floors, ceiling (顶板) and roof. It also shows the height of the bottom of the windows from the floors, and the height between the top of the doors and windows and ceiling.

If you agree with the drawings, the builder will work out an estimate (概算) of the cost of your house. He will estimate the cost of the wood (or bricks), the glass, and everything else that he must use in building the house. Later on, when he starts to build, this estimate must be corrected (修改) and revised (校正). His estimate is based on existing (目前的) prices. Prices may change, and the value (价值) of money may change, and many other things may happen between the time when he makes the estimate and the time when he builds the house.

When the builder gives you his estimate, you may wish to change your plan. (You may also wish to change your builder, if his estimate is too high.) You may find that some of the features (特色) you wanted at first cost too much, or that you can spend a little more and add something to your original plan. The builder's estimate depends on the plan, but the final plan also depends on the builder's estimate.

Reading material II

San Francisco, a City Growing up From a Devastating Earthquake and Fire

The dreadful (令人畏惧的) earthquake on 18th Aprils, 1906 destroyed the city that had grown up when men discovered gold in the deserts of California. But today the streets of San Francisco stretch over more than fourteen steep hills, rising like huge cliffs above the blue waters of the Pacific Ocean. With its hot sun and gay nightlife San Francisco is a fine place to live in or to visit. It is the most European of all American cities and you'll be sure to grow fond of it at once.

The best way to see this splendid city, where Spanish people were the first to make their homes, is to take one of the old cable cars which run along the nine main avenues. Fares are cheap; they have not risen, it is said, for almost a hundred years.

From the shop signs and the faces around you, you'll notice that in the city live people from many nations Austrians, Italians, Chinese and others giving each part a special character. More Chinese live in China Town than in any other part of the world outside China. Here, with Chinese restaurants, Chinese postboxes, and even odd telephone boxes that are like pagodas (宝塔), it is easy to feel you are in China itself.

Although the people in San Francisco prefer riding to walking, you may like to climb up the steep streets. Handrails (扶手) are provided so that you can pull yourself up. You can enjoy the splendid shops, the view from Telegraph Hill, and the houses with fountains (喷泉) and gardens. You can also look at the Stage Coach (教练), a familiar sight from Western films, which is in the window of the Wells Fargo Bank in Montgomery Street, near the business center of the city.

Wherever you walk you'll find it hard to lose yourself. At most of the important crossings there is a plan of the streets cut into the stone of the sidewalk so that you can look down and see where you are.

附录 A NEW WORDS AND PHRASES

1. accuracy	准确，精确；准确度，精度
2. accurate	精确的
3. acre	英亩(合 4,047m², 6.07 亩)
4. acronym	缩写词
5. aerospace	航天
6. aesthetically	审美地，美学观点上地
7. aluminum	铝
8. appropriate	适当的，恰当的；合适的
9. apron	窗台
10. architectural	建筑；建筑学的
11. as built	建成的，竣工的
12. asphalt	沥青
13. asset	资产
14. axis	轴向的
15. beam	梁
16. bearing wall	承重墙
17. bill of quantities	工程量清单
18. bolt	螺栓连接
19. bond	黏结
20. brace	支撑
21. brilliant	灿烂的，闪耀的，有才气的
22. broadly	广泛的
23. buddhist	佛教的
24. budget	预算
25. bulldozer	推土机，开土机，压路机
26. cable	悬索
27. calcium	钙
28. canopy	雨篷
29. cantilever	悬臂梁
30. carpenter	木匠
31. characteristic	特点，特征，特性
32. chart	图，图表；绘图，制图
33. clamshell	抓斗，蛤壳式挖泥机
34. classify	分类

35. clay	黏土
36. collapse	倒塌
37. column	柱
38. commissioner	专员；委员；长官
39. commissioning test	启用试验，试运行
40. commodity	商品
41. compact	土体压实
42. compaction	压实
43. composition	组成
44. compressive strength	抗压强度
45. compulsory	必须做的，强制性的；义务的
46. conceived	构思，以为，持有
47. conservation	保护，节约
48. constraint	强制；限制；约束
49. constructed facilities	建设设施
50. construction	建设，施工
51. construction schedule	施工计划
52. construction site	工地
53. constructional column	构造柱
54. contamination	玷污，污染，污染物
55. corrugate	弄皱，使起皱纹，起皱的，起波纹的
56. cost control	成本控制
57. cost engineering	工程估价
58. cost estimation	成本估算
59. craft	工艺，手艺
60. crane	起重机
61. criteria	标准，准则
62. critical path method	关键线路法
63. crush	压碎
64. cumulative	累积的
65. curing period	养护期
66. curriculum	课程
67. curtain wall	悬墙，幕墙
68. dead mass	自重
69. deck	甲板，舱面，桥面，层面
70. deferred	延期的，缓召的
71. derrick	悬臂式起重机
72. detonate	突然大爆炸，使爆炸
73. disastrous	损失惨重的，悲伤的
74. dismantle	拆除，拆卸，粉碎

75.	distinguish	区别，区分
76.	domain	领域
77.	dozen	（一）打，十二个
78.	dragline	拉索，拉铲挖土机
79.	duct	管道，通道，预应力筋孔
80.	ductile	易变形的
81.	ductility	延性
82.	durability	耐久性
83.	dwell	居住
84.	efficiency	效率
85.	electroosmosis	［物］电渗
86.	eminent	显赫的，杰出的，有名的，优良的
87.	enclosure	围护结构，围隔
88.	encounter	遇到，碰到
89.	endow	赋予
90.	energy-saving	节能
91.	engineering	工程；工程的
92.	enterprise	事业，计划
93.	environment	环境
94.	equipment	设备，装备
95.	erect	盖，使竖立，使直立，树立，建立
96.	evaporate	蒸发，挥发
97.	execution	实行，实施，施工
98.	exploit	开发
99.	exterior	外部的，外面的，外部，表面
100.	extrude	挤压成形
101.	facilitated	使便利；推进
102.	faculty	全体教员
103.	feasibility study	可行性研究
104.	feature	地势，地形
105.	fidelity	逼真；保真度
106.	field trip	实地考察旅行
107.	final accounts	竣工决算
108.	financing	资金筹措
109.	fine crack	微裂缝
110.	flexural	弯曲的
111.	floor	楼面
112.	footing	基脚，底座
113.	fracture	破裂，骨折
114.	fragment	断片，碎块，使成为碎片

115. frame	框架
116. framework	构架，框架结构
117. frontal	房屋正面；正面的
118. gap	缺口
119. gazetteers	地名辞典，记者，公报记者
120. geodetic	测地学的，测量的
121. grain	纹理
122. grand tour	从前英国贵族子女的遍游欧洲大陆的教育旅行
123. green building	绿色建筑
124. grid	格栅，格子
125. guarantee	保证；担保；保障；保证书
126. havoc	严重破坏
127. heritance	遗传，遗产
128. honorary	荣誉的，名誉的
129. horizontal	水平面；水平的
130. household appliance	家用电器
131. hybrid technique	混合计划方法
132. hydration	水化作用
133. immediate	直接的，紧接的，紧靠的，立即的，知觉的
134. inculcate	谆谆劝导
135. inevitable	不可避免的；必然发生的
136. infrastructure	基础设施；基础建设
137. ingredient	骨料，组分，成分，配料
138. inorganic	无机的
139. installation cost	安装工程费
140. insulation	绝热，保温，隔热
141. intelligent	聪明的；理解力强的；有智力的
142. interconversion	相互转换
143. interval（空间的）	间隔，距离，时间间隔
144. intuitively	直觉地，直观地
145. investment estimation	投资估算
146. investment quota	投资额度
147. isolated footing	独立基础
148. joint motor	马牙槎
149. kiln	（用来烧或烘干砖等的）窑，炉
150. layout	布置
151. less	减去，扣除；不计
152. lifecycle	生命周期

153.	manual	手册，指南
154.	manuscript	手稿，原稿
155.	masonry	砌体
156.	mechanism	机制，机能
157.	migration	移民，移植，移往，移动
158.	mission oriented	以目标（任务）为导向的
159.	mitigated	减轻，缓和
160.	mixer truck	混凝土搅拌车
161.	modification	修改，修正，变更，改良
162.	multidisciplinary	多学科的
163.	negligent	疏忽的；粗心大意的
164.	negligible	可以忽略的；无关紧要的；微不足道的
165.	obscurity	阴暗，朦胧，偏僻，含糊，隐匿，晦涩，身份低微
166.	observant	深切注意的
167.	opaque	不透明的，不透光的，不透明体
168.	oversight	疏忽；监督，照管；失察；负责
169.	participation	参加
170.	partition	分开，分割，隔墙，隔板
171.	perimeter wall	围墙
172.	persecution	迫害，烦扰
173.	pharmaceutical	医药的
174.	pile	桩
175.	plain concrete	素混凝土，无筋混凝土
176.	plumb	铅锤，铅弹，垂直的，使垂直，探测，垂直
177.	polystyrene foam plastic	聚苯乙烯泡沫塑料
178.	precommissioning test	启用前试验
179.	predetermined	预定的
180.	prefabrication	预先制造
181.	preliminary design estimation	初步设计概算
182.	prestressed concrete	预应力混凝土
183.	production bottleneck	生产瓶颈
184.	profile	侧面，剖面
185.	projection	投影
186.	proportion	比例
187.	pulverize	使成粉末；研磨
188.	purchase	购买；采购
189.	pursuant	追踪的；依据的

190.	raft foundation	筏板基础
191.	refractory	耐火
192.	refugee	难民，流亡者
193.	regional	地区的，区域的
194.	rehabilitated	使（身体）康复，使复职，使恢复名誉，使复原
195.	reinforced concrete	钢筋混凝土
196.	reinforcement	钢筋，加强，加固
197.	reserve fund	预备费
198.	resource	资源
199.	resource oriented	以资源为导向的
200.	ring beam	圈梁
201.	rivet	铆接
202.	scenarios	情景
203.	schedule	进度
204.	scraper	铲运机，刮土机，平土机
205.	section	剖面
206.	sequencing	先后顺序；定序
207.	set forth	阐明，宣布，提出，陈列，出发，把（会议等）提前
208.	sexagesima	六十的，六十进位的，以六十为分母的分数
209.	shear	剪切，剪力
210.	sheet	薄板
211.	shell	壳体
212.	shovel	铲，挖掘机，单斗挖土机
213.	shrinkage	收缩
214.	silt	粉土
215.	skeleton	骨架
216.	slab	板
217.	soaring	猛增的
218.	solidify	固化，固结，凝固
219.	spiral	螺旋形的
220.	spread foundation	扩展基础
221.	stability	稳定性
222.	stadia	视距，视距仪器，stadium 的复数
223.	stilt floor	架空层
224.	stirrup	箍筋
225.	straightedge	直缘（棱）的，直规的
226.	strata	stratum 的复数，层，地层，阶层

227.	stratification	层理；成层
228.	structural calculation	结构计算
229.	structure	结构
230.	superstructure	上部结构
231.	supervise	监督，管理，指导
232.	supervision	监督；管理
233.	sustainable design	可持续设计
234.	synthesized	被组合
235.	taking over	接任，接管，验收
236.	talented	有才能的
237.	tension	拉力，张力
238.	terminology	术语学
239.	theodolite	［测］精密经纬仪
240.	three-dimensional	三维的
241.	time oriented	以时间为导向的
242.	tow	拖，拉，牵引
243.	transfer	传递
244.	triangle	三角形
245.	tripod	三脚桌，三脚架
246.	truss	桁架
247.	tuberculosis	肺结核
248.	unrelenting	无情的；冷酷的
249.	validate	使合法化；使生效；批准
250.	veil wall	幕墙
251.	ventilation	通风、换气
252.	vibratory-type roller	振动碾
253.	weld	焊接
254.	well point	降低地下水位的井点，深坑点

附录B 建筑工程常用术语翻译及名词解释

B1 一般术语

1. 工程结构 building and civil engineering structures

房屋建筑和土木工程的建筑物、构筑物及其相关组成部分的总称。

2. 工程结构设计 design of building and civil engineering structures

在工程结构的可靠与经济、适用与美观之间,选择一种最佳的合理的平衡,使所建造的结构能满足各种预定功能要求。

3. 房屋建筑工程 building engineering

一般称为建筑工程,是指为新建、改建或扩建房屋建筑物和附属构筑物所进行的勘察、规划、设计、施工、安装和维护等各项技术工作和完成的工程实体。

4. 土木工程 civil engineering

除房屋建筑外,为新建、改建或扩建各类工程的建筑物、构筑物和相关配套设施等所进行的勘察、规划、设计、施工、安装和维护等各项技术工作和完成的工程实体。

5. 建筑物(构筑物) construction works

房屋建筑或土木工程中的单项工程实体。

6. 结构 structure

广义指房屋建筑和土木工程的建筑物、构筑物及其相关组成部分的实体,狭义指各种工程实体的承重骨架。

7. 基础 foundation

将建筑物、构筑物以及各种设施的上部结构所承受的各种作用和自重传递到地基的结构组成部分。

8. 地基 foundation soil; subgrade; subbase; ground

支承由基础传递或直接由上部结构传递的各种作用的土体或岩体。未经加工处理的称为天然地基。

9. 木结构 timber structure

以木材为主制作的结构。

10. 砌体结构 masonry structure

以砌体为主制作的结构。它包括砖结构、石结构和其他材料的砌块结构。砌体结构分为无筋砌体结构和配筋砌体结构。

11. 钢结构 steel structure

以钢材为主制作的结构。其中由带钢或钢板经冷加工形成的型材所制作的结构称为冷弯薄壁型钢结构。

12. 混凝土(砼)结构 concrete structure

以混凝土为主制作的结构。它包括素混凝土结构、钢筋混凝土结构和预应力混凝土结构等。

13. 特种工程结构 special engineering structure

指具有特种用途的建筑物、构筑物，如高耸结构，包括塔、烟囱、桅、海洋平台、容器、构架等各种结构。

14. 房屋建筑 building

在固定地点，为使用者或占用物提供用以进行生活、生产或进行其他活动场所的实体。

15. 工业建筑 industrial building

提供生产用的各种建筑物，如车间、厂前区建筑、生活间、动力站、库房和运输设施等。

16. 民用建筑 civil building; civil architecture

指非生产性的居住建筑和公共建筑，如住宅、办公楼、幼儿园、学校、食堂、影剧院、商店、体育馆、旅馆、医院、展览馆等。

B2 房屋建筑结构术语

1. 混合结构 mixed structure

不同材料的构件或部件混合组成的结构。

2. 板柱结构 slab-column system

由楼板和柱(无梁)组成承重体系的房屋结构，如升板结构、无梁楼盖结构、整体预应力板柱结构。

3. 框架结构 frame structure

由梁柱组成的能承受竖向、水平方向作用所产生的各种效应的单层、多层或高层结构。

4. 拱结构 arch structure

由拱作为承重体系的结构。

5. 折板结构 folded-plate structure

由多块条形或其他外形的平板组合而成,能作承重、围护用的薄壁空间结构。

6. 壳体结构 shell structure

由各种形状的曲面板与边缘构件(梁、拱、桁架)组成的大跨度覆盖或围护的空间结构。

7. 空间网架结构 space truss structure

由多根杆件按一定网格形式通过节点连接而形成的大跨度覆盖的空间结构。

8. 悬索结构 cable-suspended structure

由柔性受拉索及其边缘构件所组成的承重结构。

9. 充气结构 pneumatic structure

在以高分子材料制成的薄膜制品中充入空气后而形成房屋的结构。充气结构分气承式和气管式两种结构形式。

10. 剪力墙(结构墙)结构 shear wall structure

在高层和多层建筑中,竖向和水平方向作用均由钢筋混凝土或预应力混凝土墙体承受的结构。

11. 框架-剪力墙结构 frame-shear wall structure

在高层建筑或工业厂房中,剪力墙和框架共同承受竖向和水平方向作用的一种组合型结构。

12. 筒体结构 tube structure

由竖向箱形截面悬臂筒体组成的结构。筒体有剪力墙围成竖向箱形截面的薄壁筒和密柱框架组成竖向箱形截面的框筒。筒体由一个或多个组成,分为筒中筒、单框筒、框架-薄壁筒和成束筒4类。

13. 悬挂结构 suspended structure

将楼(屋)面系统的荷载通过吊杆传递到悬挂的水平桁架(梁),再由悬挂的水平桁架(梁)传递到被悬挂的井筒上直至基础的结构。

14. 高耸结构 high-rise structure

高度大,水平横向剖面相对较小,并以水平荷载控制设计的结构,分自立式塔式结构和拉线式桅式结构两大类,如水塔、烟囱、电视塔、监测塔等。

B3 结构构件和部件术语

1. 构件 member

组成结构的单元。

2. 部件 component；assembly parts

结构中由若干构件组成的组合件，如楼梯、阳台、楼盖等。

3. 截面 section

设计时所考虑的结构构件与某一平面的交面。当该交面与结构构件的纵向轴线或中面正交时的面称为正截面，斜交时的面称为斜截面。

4. 梁 beam；girder

一种由支座支承的直线或曲线形构件。它主要承受各种作用产生的弯矩和剪力，有时也承受扭矩。

5. 拱 arch

一种由支座支承的曲线或折线形构件。它主要承受各种作用产生的轴向压力，有时也承受弯矩、剪力或扭矩。

6. 板 slab；plate

一种由支座支承的平面尺寸大而厚度相对较小的平面构件。它主要承受各种作用产生的弯矩和剪力。

7. 壳 shell

一种曲面构件。它主要承受各种作用产生的中面内的力，有时也承受弯矩、剪力或扭矩。

8. 柱 column

一种竖向直线构件。它主要承受各种作用产生的轴向压力，有时也承受弯矩、剪力或扭矩。

9. 墙 wall

一种竖向平面或曲面构件。它主要承受各种作用产生的中面内的力，有时也承受中面外的弯矩和剪力。

10. 桁架 truss

由若干杆件构成的一种平面或空间的格架式结构或构件。各杆件主要承受各种作用产生的轴向力，有时也承受节点弯矩和剪力。

11. 框架 frame

由梁和柱连接而构成的一种平面或空间、单层或多层的结构。

12. 排架 bent frame

由梁（或桁架）和柱铰接而成的单层框架。

13. 刚架（刚构）rigid frame

由梁和柱刚接而构成的框架。

14. 简支梁 simply supported beam

将梁搁置在两端支座上，其一端为轴向有约束的铰支座，另一端为能轴向滚动的支座。

15. 悬臂梁 cantilever beam

梁的一端为不产生轴向、垂直位移和转动的固定支座，另一端为自由端。

16. 两端固定梁 beam fixed at both ends

梁的两端均为不产生轴向、垂直位移和转动的固定支座。

17. 连续梁 continuous beam

具有3个或3个以上支座的梁。

18. 叠合梁 superposed beam

截面由同一材料若干部分重叠而成为整体的梁。

19. 桩 pile

沉入、打入或浇注于地基中的柱状支承构件，如木桩、钢桩、混凝土桩等。

20. 板桩 sheet pile

全部或部分打入地基中，横截面为长方板形的支承构件，如钢板桩、钢筋混凝土板桩。

21. 护坡 slope protection；revetment

为防止边坡受水冲刷，在坡面上所做的各种铺砌和栽植的统称。

22. 挡土墙 retaining wall

主要承受土压力，防止土体塌滑的墙式建筑物。

23. 连接 connection

构件间或杆件间以某种方式的结合。

24. 节点 joint

构件或杆件相互连接的部位。

25. 伸缩缝 expansion and contraction joint

为减轻材料胀缩变形对建筑物的影响而在建筑物中预先设置的间隙。

26. 沉降缝 settlement joint

为减轻地基不均匀变形对建筑物的影响而在建筑物中预先设置的间隙。

27. 防震缝 aseismic joint

为减轻或防止相邻结构单元由地震作用引起的碰撞而预先设置的间隙。

28. 施工缝 construction joint

当混凝土施工时，由于技术上或施工组织上的原因不能一次连续灌注时，而在结构的规定位置留置的搭接面或后浇带。

B4 地基和基础术语

1. 扩展(扩大)基础 spread foundation

将块石或混凝土砌筑的截面适当扩大,以适应地基容许承载能力或变形的天然地基基础。

2. 刚性基础 rigid foundation

基础底部扩展部分不超过基础材料刚性角的天然地基基础。

3. 独立基础 single footing

用于单柱下并按材料和受力状态选定形式的基础。

4. 联合基础 combined footing

有两根或两根以上的立柱(筒体)共用的基础,或两种不同形式基础共同工作的基础。

5. 条形基础 strip foundation

水平长而狭的带状基础。

6. 壳体基础 shell foundation

以壳体结构形成的空间薄壁基础。

7. 箱形基础 box foundation

由钢筋混凝土底板、顶板侧墙板和一定数量的内隔墙板组成整体的形似箱形的基础。

8. 筏形基础 raft foundation

支承整个建筑物或构筑物的大面积整体钢筋混凝土板式或梁板式基础。

9. 桩基础 pile foundation

由桩连接桩顶、桩帽和承台组成的深基础。

10. 沉井基础 open caisson foundation

上下敞口带刃脚的空心井筒状结构下沉水中到设计标高处,以井筒作为结构外壳而建筑成的基础。

11. 管柱基础 cylinder pile foundation;cylinder caisson foundation

大直径钢筋混凝土或预应力混凝土圆管,用人工或机械清除管内土、石,下沉至地基中,用于岩层或坚实地层的基础。

12. 沉箱基础 caisson foundation

用气压排水,开挖水下土(岩)层,把闭口箱下沉到设计标高所建成的基础。

B5 结构上的作用、作用代表值和作用效应术语

1. 作用 action

施加在结构上的一组集中力或分布力，或引起结构外加变形或约束变形的原因。前者称为直接作用，后者称为间接作用。

2. 荷载 load

指施加在结构上的集中力或分布力。

3. 线分布力 force per unit length

施加在结构或构件单位长度上的力。

4. 面分布力 force per unit area

施加在结构或构件单位面积上的力，也称为压强。

5. 体分布力 force per unit volume

施加在结构或构件单位体积上的力。

6. 力矩 moment of force

力与力臂的乘积。

7. 永久作用 permanent action

在设计基准期内量值不随时间变化的作用，或其变化与平均值相比可以忽略不计的作用，其中，直接作用也称为恒荷载。

8. 可变作用 variable action

在设计基准期内量值随时间变化且其变化与平均值相比不可以忽略的作用，其中，直接作用也称为活荷载。

9. 偶然作用 accidental action

在设计基准期内不一定出现而一旦出现其量值很大且持续时间较短的作用。

10. 固定作用 fixed action

在结构上具有固定分布的作用。

11. 自重 self weight

指材料自身重量产生的重力。

12. 施工荷载 site load

在施工阶段施加在结构或构件上的临时荷载。

13. 土压力 earth pressure

土体作用在建筑物或构筑物上的力，促使建筑物或构筑物移动的土体推

力称为主动土压力；阻止建筑物或构筑物移动的土体对抗力称为被动土压力。

14. 温度作用 temperature action

结构或构件受外部或内部条件约束，当外界温度变化时或在有温差的条件下，不能自由胀缩而产生的作用。

15. 地震作用 earthquake action

由地运动引起的结构动态作用，分水平地震作用和竖向地震作用，设计时根据其超越概率，可视为可变作用或偶然作用。

16. 爆炸作用 explosion action

由爆炸通过空气、岩土产生的冲击波、压缩波等而引起的结构的动态作用。

17. 风荷载 wind load

作用在建筑物上或构筑物表面上计算用的风压。

18. 雪荷载 snow load

作用在建筑物或构筑物顶面上计算用的雪压。

19. 吊车荷载 crane load

工业建筑用的吊车起吊重物时对建筑物产生计算用的竖向作用或水平作用。

20. 楼面、屋面活荷载 floor live load；roof live load

楼面或屋面上计算用的直接作用，通常以等效的面分布力表示。

21. 轴向力 normal force

作用引起的结构或构件某一正截面上的法向拉力或压力，当法向力位于截面形心时，称为轴心力(axial force)。

22. 剪力 shear force

作用引起的结构或构件某一截面上的切向力。

23. 弯矩 bending moment

作用引起的结构或构件某一截面上的内力矩。

24. 扭矩 torque

作用引起的结构或构件某一截面上的剪力所构成的力偶矩。

25. 应力 stress

作用引起的结构或构件中某一截面单位面积上的力。

26. 正应力 normal stress

作用引起的结构或构件某一截面单位面积上的法向拉力或压力。前者称为拉应力，后者称为压应力。

27. 剪应力 shear stress; tangential stress

作用引起的结构或构件某一截面单位面积上的切向力。

28. 预应力 prestress

在结构或构件承受其他作用前预先施加的作用所产生的应力。

29. 位移 displacement

作用引起的结构或构件中某点位置的改变，或某线段方向的改变。前者称为线位移，后者称为角位移。

30. 挠度 deflection

在弯矩作用平面内，结构构件轴线或中面上某点由挠曲引起垂直于轴线或中面方向的线位移。

31. 变形 deformation

作用引起的结构或构件中各点间的相对位移。

32. 应变 strain

作用引起的结构或构件中的各种应力所产生的相应的单位变形。

B6　材料性能、构件承载能力和材料性能代表值术语

1. 抗力 resistance

结构或构件及其材料承受作用效应的能力，如承载能力、刚度、抗裂度、强度等。

2. 强度 strength

材料抵抗破坏的能力。其值为在一定的受力状态或工作条件下，材料所能承受的最大应力。

3. 抗压强度 compressive strength

材料所能承受的最大压应力。

4. 抗拉强度 tensile strength

材料所能承受的最大拉应力。

5. 抗剪强度 shear strength

材料所能承受的最大剪应力。

6. 抗弯强度 flexural strength

在受弯状态下材料所能承受的最大拉应力或压应力。

7. 屈服强度 yield strength

钢材在受力过程中荷载不增加或略有降低而变形持续增加时所受的恒定

应力。对于受拉无明显屈服现象的钢材，则为标距部分残余伸长达原标距长度0.2%时的应力。

8. 极限应变 ultimate strain

材料受力后相应于最大应力的应变。

9. 弹性模量 modulus of elasticity

材料在单向受拉或受压且应力和应变呈线性关系时，截面上正应力与对应的正应变的比值。

10. 承载能力 bearing capacity

结构或构件所能承受的最大内力，或达到不适于继续承载的变形时的内力。

11. 受压承载能力 compressive capacity

构件所能承受的最大轴向压力，或达到不适于继续承载的变形时的轴向压力。

12. 受拉承载能力 tensile capacity

构件所能承受的最大轴向拉力，或达到不适于继续承载的变形时的轴向拉力。

13. 受剪承载能力 shear capacity

构件所能承受的最大剪力，或达到不适于继续承载的变形时的剪力。

14. 受弯承载能力 flexural capacity

构件所能承受的最大弯矩，或达到不适于继续承载的变形时的弯矩。

15. 受扭承载能力 torsional capacity

构件所能承受的最大扭矩，或达到不适于继续承载的变形时的扭矩。

16. 刚度 stiffness；rigidity

结构或构件抵抗单位变形的能力。

17. 稳定性 stability

结构或构件保持稳定状态的能力。

18. 脆性破坏 brittle failure

结构或构件在破坏前无明显变形或其他预兆的破坏类型。

19. 延性破坏 ductile failure

结构或构件在破坏前有明显变形或其他预兆的破坏类型。

B7 几何参数和常用量术语

1. 截面高度 height of section; depth of section

一般指构件正截面在弯矩作用平面上的投影长度。

2. 截面宽度 breadth of section

一般指构件正截面在与高度相垂直的方向上的某一尺寸。

3. 截面厚度 thickness of section

一般指构件薄壁部分截面边缘间的尺寸。

4. 截面直径 diameter of section

圆形截面通过圆心的弦长。

5. 截面周长 perimeter of section

截面边缘线的总长度。

6. 截面面积 area of section

截面边缘线所包围的材料平面面积。

7. 截面面积矩 first moment of area

截面各微元面积与微元至截面上某一指定轴线距离乘积的积分。

8. 截面惯性矩 second moment of area; moment of inertia

截面各微元面积与各微元至截面上某一指定轴线距离二次方乘积的积分。

9. 截面模量(抵抗矩) section modulus

截面对其形心轴的惯性矩与截面上最远点至形心轴距离的比值。

10. 截面回转半径 radius of gyration

截面对其形心轴的惯性矩除以截面面积的商的正二次方根。

11. 偏心矩 eccentricity

偏心受力构件中轴向力作用点至截面形心的距离。

12. 长度 length

结构或构件长轴方向的尺寸。

13. 跨度 span

结构或构件两相邻支承间的距离。

14. 长细比 slenderness ratio

构件的计算长度与其截面回转半径的比值。

B8 结构抗震术语

1. 振动 vibration

物体反复通过某个基准位置的运动。

2. 加速度 acceleration

速度变化与发生这一变化所经过的时间的比,即单位时间内速度的变化。

3. 频率 frequency

物体每秒振动的次数。

4. 地震 earthquake

地球内部运动的累积使岩层剧烈振动,并以波的形式向地表传播而引起地面的颠簸和摇晃。

5. 震源 earthquake focus

地震发生时在地球内部产生地震波的位置。

6. 震中 earthquake epicentre

震源在地面上的垂直投影点。

7. 震中距 epicentral distance

在地震影响范围内,地表某处与震中的距离。

8. 地震震级 earthquake magnitude

衡量一次地震所释放的能量大小的尺度。

9. 地震烈度 earthquake intensity

地震对地表及工程建筑物影响的强弱程度。

10. 地震区 earthquake zone

经常发生地震的地区或地震能引起工程结构破坏的地区。

11. 砂土液化 liquefaction of saturated soil

地震时饱和砂土的承载能力消失,导致地面沉陷、斜坡失稳或地基失效。

B9 常用施工术语

1. 施工缝 construction joint

在混凝土浇筑过程中,因设计要求或施工需要分段浇筑而在先、后浇筑的混凝土之间所形成的接缝。

2. 缺陷 defect

建筑工程施工质量中不符合规定要求的检验项或检验点,按其程度可分为严重缺陷和一般缺陷。

3. 严重缺陷 serious defect

对结构构件的受力性能或安装使用性能有决定性影响的缺陷。

4. 检验 inspection

对被检验项目的特征、性能进行量测、检查、试验等,并将结果与标准规定的要求进行比较,以确定项目每项性能是否合格的活动。

5. 进场检验 site inspection

对进入施工现场的建造材料、性能进行量测、检查、试验等,并将结果与标准规定的要求进行比较,以确定项目每项性能是否合格的活动。

6. 见证检验 evidential testing

施工单位在工程监理单位或建设单位的见证下,按照有关规定从施工现场随机抽取试样,送至具备相应资质的检测机构进行检验的活动。

7. 复验 repeat test

建筑材料、设备等进入施工现场后,在外观质量检查和质量证明文件核查符合要求的基础上,按照有关规定从施工现场抽取试样送至实验室进行检验的活动。

8. 检验批 inspection lot

按相同的生产条件或按规定的方式汇总起来供抽样检验用的,由一定数量样本组成的检验体。

9. 验收 acceptance

建筑工程质量在施工单位自行检查合格的基础上,由工程质量验收责任方组织,工程建设相关单位参加,对检验批、分项、分部、单位工程及其隐蔽工程的质量进行抽样检验,对技术文件进行审核,并根据设计文件和相关标准以书面形式对工程质量是否达到合格作出确认。

10. 主控项目 dominant item

建筑工程中对安全、节能、环境保护和主要使用功能起决定性作用的检验项目。

11. 一般项目 general item

除主控项目以外的检验项目。

12. 抽样方案 sampling scheme

根据检验项目的特性所确定的抽样数量和方法。

13. 观感质量 quality of appearance

通过观察和必要的测试所反映的工程外在质量和功能状态。

14. 返修 repair

对施工质量不符合标准规定的部位采取的整修等措施。

15. 返工 rework

对施工质量不符合标准规定的部位采取的更换、重新制作、重新施工等措施。

参 考 文 献

[1] [美] E. J. 霍尔. 土木工程英语读本 [M]. 俞天玫, 译. 北京: 中国建筑工业出版社, 1984.
[2] B. Austin Barry. *Construction Measurements* [M]. USA: John Wiley and Sons Ltd, 1988.
[3] 邓贤贵. 建筑工程英语 [M]. 武汉: 华中科技大学出版社, 1997.
[4] 段兵廷. 土木工程专业英语 [M]. 武汉: 武汉理工大学出版社, 2003.
[5] 高湘. 给水排水工程专业(高等学校专业英语系列教材) [M]. 北京: 中国建筑工业出版社, 2006.
[6] 贾艳敏. 土木工程专业英语 [M]. 北京: 科学出版社, 2005.
[7] 姜海燕. 建筑专业英语 [M]. 北京: 中国建材工业出版社, 2003.
[8] 刘剑. 电气工程及自动化专业英语 [M]. 北京: 中国电力出版社, 2004.
[9] 裴玉龙. 交通工程专业英语 [M]. 北京: 人民交通出版社, 2002.
[10] 钱永梅, 庞平. 土木工程专业英语(建筑工程方向) [M]. 北京: 化学工业出版社, 2008.
[11] 孙清娟, 陈慧. 测绘专业英语 [M]. 郑州: 黄河水利出版社, 2006.
[12] 汪德华. 建筑工程专业英语 [M]. 北京: 地震出版社, 2003.
[13] 徐勇戈, 等. 工程管理专业英语 [M]. 北京: 中国建筑工业出版社, 2006.
[14] 赵明瑜. 土木建筑系列英语第三级 [M]. 北京: 中国建筑工业出版社, 1987.
[15] 赵明瑜. 土木建筑系列英语第四级 [M]. 北京: 中国建筑工业出版社, 1987.
[16] 赵研. 建造构造 [M]. 北京: 中国建筑工业出版社, 2000.
[17] 周开鑫. 土木类工程英语(教程) [M]. 北京: 人民交通出版社, 2001.
[18] 顾惠民. 土木建筑系列英语第二级 [M]. 北京: 中国建筑工业出版社, 1987.
[19] 韦成秀. 建筑英语 [M]. 北京: 中国建筑工业出版社, 1997.
[20] 郭向荣, 陈政清. 土木工程专业英语 [M]. 北京: 中国铁道出版社, 2001.
[21] 李著景. 初等钢筋混凝土结构 [M]. 北京: 清华大学出版社, 2005.
[22] 吕广华, 陈颢. 建筑工程基础(上) [M]. 武汉: 中国地质大学出版社, 2005.
[23] 陈书申, 陈晓平. 土力学与地基基础 [M]. 武汉: 武汉理工大学出版社, 2006.
[24] 杨匡汉. 土木建筑系列英语第一级 [M]. 北京: 中国建筑工业出版社, 1987.
[25] 马彩玲. 土木工程英语 [M]. 北京: 清华大学出版社, 北京交通大学出版社, 2011.
[26] 璩继立, 宿晓萍. 土木工程专业英语 [M]. 北京: 中国电力出版社, 2014.
[27] 徐勇戈. 工程管理专业英语 [M]. 北京: 中国建筑工业出版社, 2014.

北京大学出版社高职高专土建系列教材书目

序号	书　名	书　号	编著者	定价	出版时间	配套情况
	"互联网+"创新规划教材					
1	建筑构造(第二版)	978-7-301-26480-5	肖　芳	42.00	2016.1	ppt/APP/二维码
2	建筑装饰构造(第二版)	978-7-301-26572-7	赵志文等	39.50	2016.1	ppt/二维码
3	建筑工程概论	978-7-301-25934-4	申淑荣等	40.00	2015.8	ppt/二维码
4	市政管道工程施工	978-7-301-26629-8	雷彩虹	46.00	2016.5	ppt/二维码
5	市政道路工程施工	978-7-301-26632-8	张雪丽	49.00	2016.5	ppt/二维码
6	建筑三维平法结构图集(第二版)	978-7-301-29049-1	傅华夏	68.00	2018.1	APP
7	建筑三维平法结构识图教程(第二版)	978-7-301-29121-4	傅华夏	68.00	2018.1	APP/ppt
8	建筑工程制图与识图(第2版)	978-7-301-24408-1	白丽红	34.00	2016.8	APP/二维码
9	建筑设备基础知识与识图(第2版)	978-7-301-24586-6	靳慧征等	47.00	2016.8	二维码
10	建筑结构基础与识图	978-7-301-27215-2	周　晖	58.00	2016.9	ppt/二维码
11	建筑构造与识图	978-7-301-27838-3	孙　伟	40.00	2017.1	APP/二维码
12	建筑工程施工技术(第三版)	978-7-301-27675-4	钟汉华等	66.00	2016.11	APP/二维码
13	工程建设监理案例分析教程(第二版)	978-7-301-27864-2	刘志麟等	50.00	2017.1	ppt/二维码
14	建筑工程质量与安全管理(第二版)	978-7-301-27219-0	郑　伟	55.00	2016.8	ppt/二维码
15	建筑工程计量与计价——透过案例学造价(第2版)	978-7-301-23852-3	张　强	59.00	2014.4	ppt/二维码
16	城乡规划原理与设计(原城市规划原理与设计)	978-7-301-27771-3	谭婧婧等	43.00	2017.1	ppt/素材/二维码
17	建筑工程计量与计价	978-7-301-27866-6	吴育萍等	49.00	2017.1	ppt/二维码
18	建筑工程计量与计价(第3版)	978-7-301-25344-1	肖明和等	65.00	2017.1	APP/二维码
19	市政工程计量与计价(第三版)	978-7-301-27983-0	郭良娟等	59.00	2017.2	ppt/二维码
20	高层建筑施工	978-7-301-28232-8	吴俊臣	65.00	2017.4	ppt/答案
21	建筑施工机械(第二版)	978-7-301-28247-2	吴志强等	35.00	2017.5	ppt/答案
22	市政工程概论	978-7-301-28260-1	郭　福等	46.00	2017.5	ppt/二维码
23	建筑工程测量(第二版)	978-7-301-28296-0	石　东等	51.00	2017.5	ppt/二维码
24	工程项目招投标与合同管理(第三版)	978-7-301-28439-1	周艳冬	44.00	2017.7	ppt/二维码
25	建筑制图(第三版)	978-7-301-28411-7	高丽荣	38.00	2017.7	ppt/APP/二维码
26	建筑制图习题集(第三版)	978-7-301-27897-0	高丽荣	35.00	2017.7	APP
27	建筑力学(第三版)	978-7-301-28600-5	刘明晖	55.00	2017.8	ppt/二维码
28	中外建筑史(第三版)	978-7-301-28689-0	袁新华等	42.00	2017.9	ppt/二维码
29	建筑施工技术	978-7-301-28575-6	陈雄辉	54.00	2018.1	ppt/二维码
30	建筑工程经济(第三版)	978-7-301-28723-1	张宁宁等	36.00	2017.9	ppt/答案/二维码
31	建筑材料与检测	978-7-301-28809-2	陈玉萍	44.00	2017.10	ppt/二维码
32	建筑识图与构造	978-7-301-28876-4	林秋怡等	46.00	2017.11	ppt/二维码
32	建筑工程材料	978-7-301-28982-2	向积波等	42.00	2018.1	ppt/二维码
33	建筑力学与结构(少学时版)(第二版)	978-7-301-29022-4	吴承霞等	46.00	2017.12	ppt/答案
34	建筑工程测量(第三版)	978-7-301-29113-9	张敬伟等	49.00	2018.1	ppt/答案/二维码
35	建筑工程测量实验与实训指导(第三版)	978-7-301-29112-2	张敬伟等	29.00	2018.1	答案/二维码
36	安装工程计量与计价(第四版)	978-7-301-16737-3	冯钢	59.00	2018.1	ppt/答案/二维码
37	建筑工程施工组织设计(第二版)	978-7-301-29130-0	鄢维峰等	37.00	2018.1	ppt/答案/二维码
38	建筑工程测量	978-7-301-28757-6	赵　昕	50.00	2018.1	ppt/二维码
39	建筑材料与检测(第2版)	978-7-301-25347-2	梅　杨等	35.00	2015.2	ppt/答案/二维码
	"十二五"职业教育国家规划教材					
1	★建筑工程应用文写作(第2版)	978-7-301-24480-7	赵立等	50.00	2014.8	ppt
2	★土木工程实用力学(第2版)	978-7-301-24681-8	马景善	47.00	2015.7	ppt
3	★建设工程监理(第2版)	978-7-301-24490-6	斯　庆	35.00	2015.1	ppt/答案
4	★建筑节能工程与施工	978-7-301-24274-2	吴明军等	35.00	2015.5	ppt
5	★建筑工程经济(第2版)	978-7-301-24492-0	胡六星等	41.00	2014.9	ppt/答案
6	★建设工程招投标与合同管理(第3版)	978-7-301-24483-8	宋春岩	40.00	2014.9	ppt/答案/试题/教案
7	★工程造价概论	978-7-301-24696-2	周艳冬	31.00	2015.1	ppt/答案
8	★建筑工程计量与计价(第3版)	978-7-301-25344-1	肖明和等	65.00	2017.1	APP/二维码
9	★建筑工程计量与计价实训(第3版)	978-7-301-25345-8	肖明和等	29.00	2015.7	
10	★建筑装饰施工技术(第2版)	978-7-301-24482-1	王　军	37.00	2014.7	ppt
11	★工程地质与土力学(第2版)	978-7-301-24479-1	杨仲元	41.00	2014.7	ppt
	基础课程					
1	建设法规及相关知识	978-7-301-22748-0	唐茂华等	34.00	2013.9	ppt
2	建设工程法规(第2版)	978-7-301-24493-7	皇甫婧琪	40.50	2014.8	ppt/答案/素材

序号	书　名	书　号	编著者	定价	出版时间	配套情况
3	建筑工程法规实务(第2版)	978-7-301-26188-0	杨陈慧等	49.50	2017.6	ppt
4	建筑法规	978-7-301-19371-6	董伟等	39.00	2011.9	ppt
5	建设工程法规	978-7-301-20912-7	王先恕	32.00	2012.7	ppt
6	AutoCAD 建筑制图教程(第2版)	978-7-301-21095-6	郭慧	38.00	2013.3	ppt/素材
7	AutoCAD 建筑绘图教程(第2版)	978-7-301-24540-8	唐英敏等	44.00	2014.7	ppt
8	建筑CAD项目教程(2010版)	978-7-301-20979-0	郭慧	38.00	2012.9	素材
9	建筑工程专业英语(第二版)	978-7-301-26597-0	吴承霞	24.00	2016.2	ppt
10	建筑工程专业英语	978-7-301-20003-2	韩薇等	24.00	2012.2	ppt
11	建筑识图与构造(第2版)	978-7-301-23774-8	郑贵超	40.00	2014.2	ppt/答案
12	房屋建筑构造	978-7-301-19883-4	李少红	26.00	2012.1	ppt
13	建筑识图	978-7-301-21893-8	邓志勇等	35.00	2013.1	ppt
14	建筑识图与房屋构造	978-7-301-22860-9	贠禄等	54.00	2013.9	ppt/答案
15	建筑构造与设计	978-7-301-23506-5	陈玉萍	38.00	2014.1	ppt/答案
16	房屋建筑构造	978-7-301-23588-1	李元玲等	45.00	2014.1	ppt
17	房屋建筑构造习题集	978-7-301-26005-0	李元玲	26.00	2015.8	ppt/答案
18	建筑构造与施工图识读	978-7-301-24470-8	南学平	52.00	2014.8	ppt
19	建筑工程识图实训教程	978-7-301-26057-9	孙伟	32.00	2015.12	ppt
20	◎建筑工程制图与识图(第2版)	978-7-301-24408-1	白丽红	34.00	2016.8	APP/二维码
21	建筑制图习题集(第2版)	978-7-301-24571-2	白丽红	25.00	2014.8	
22	◎建筑工程制图(第2版)(附习题册)	978-7-301-21120-5	肖明和	48.00	2012.8	ppt
23	建筑制图与识图(第2版)	978-7-301-24386-2	曹雪梅	38.00	2015.8	ppt
24	建筑制图与识图习题册	978-7-301-18652-7	曹雪梅等	30.00	2011.4	
25	建筑制图与识图(第二版)	978-7-301-25834-7	李元玲	32.00	2016.9	ppt
26	建筑制图与识图习题集	978-7-301-20425-2	李元玲	24.00	2012.3	ppt
27	新编建筑工程制图	978-7-301-21140-3	方筱松	30.00	2012.8	ppt
28	新编建筑工程制图习题集	978-7-301-16834-9	方筱松	22.00	2012.8	
建筑施工类						
1	建筑工程测量	978-7-301-19992-3	潘益民	38.00	2012.2	ppt
2	建筑工程测量	978-7-301-13578-5	王金玲等	26.00	2008.5	
3	建筑工程测量实训(第2版)	978-7-301-24833-1	杨凤华	34.00	2015.3	答案
4	建筑工程测量	978-7-301-22485-4	景铎等	34.00	2013.6	
5	建筑施工技术	978-7-301-12336-2	朱永祥等	38.00	2008.8	ppt
6	建筑施工技术	978-7-301-16726-7	叶雯等	44.00	2010.8	ppt/素材
7	建筑施工技术	978-7-301-19499-7	董伟等	42.00	2011.9	ppt
8	建筑施工技术	978-7-301-19997-8	苏小梅	38.00	2012.1	ppt
9	建筑施工机械	978-7-301-19365-5	吴志强	30.00	2011.10	ppt
10	基础工程施工	978-7-301-20917-2	董伟等	35.00	2012.7	ppt
11	建筑施工技术实训(第2版)	978-7-301-24368-8	周晓龙	30.00	2014.7	
12	土木工程力学	978-7-301-16864-6	吴明军	38.00	2010.4	ppt
13	PKPM软件的应用(第2版)	978-7-301-22625-4	王娜等	34.00	2013.6	
14	◎建筑结构(第2版)(上册)	978-7-301-21106-9	徐锡权	41.00	2013.4	ppt/答案
15	◎建筑结构(第2版)(下册)	978-7-301-22584-4	徐锡权	42.00	2013.6	ppt/答案
16	建筑结构学习指导与技能训练(上册)	978-7-301-25929-0	徐锡权	28.00	2015.8	ppt
17	建筑结构学习指导与技能训练(下册)	978-7-301-25933-7	徐锡权	28.00	2015.8	ppt
18	建筑结构	978-7-301-19171-2	唐春平等	41.00	2011.8	ppt
19	建筑结构基础	978-7-301-21125-0	王中发	36.00	2012.8	ppt
20	建筑结构原理及应用	978-7-301-18732-6	史美东	45.00	2012.8	ppt
21	建筑结构与识图	978-7-301-26935-0	相秉志	37.00	2016.2	
22	建筑力学与结构(第2版)	978-7-301-22148-8	吴承霞等	49.00	2013.4	ppt/答案
23	建筑力学与结构	978-7-301-20988-2	陈水广	32.00	2012.8	ppt
24	建筑力学与结构	978-7-301-23348-1	杨丽君等	44.00	2014.1	ppt
25	建筑结构与施工图	978-7-301-22188-4	朱希文等	35.00	2013.3	ppt
26	生态建筑材料	978-7-301-19588-2	陈剑峰等	38.00	2011.10	ppt
27	建筑材料(第2版)	978-7-301-24633-7	林祖宏	35.00	2014.8	ppt
28	建筑材料检测试验指导	978-7-301-16729-8	王美芬等	18.00	2010.10	
29	建筑材料与检测(第二版)	978-7-301-26550-5	王辉	40.00	2016.1	ppt
30	建筑材料与检测试验指导(第二版)	978-7-301-28471-1	王辉	23.00	2017.7	ppt
31	建筑材料选择与应用	978-7-301-21948-5	申淑荣等	39.00	2013.3	ppt
32	建筑材料检测实训	978-7-301-22317-0	申淑荣等	24.00	2013.4	
33	建筑材料	978-7-301-24208-7	任晓菲	40.00	2014.7	ppt/答案
34	建筑材料检测试验指导	978-7-301-24782-2	陈东佐等	20.00	2014.9	ppt
35	◎建设工程监理概论(第2版)	978-7-301-20854-0	徐锡权等	43.00	2012.8	ppt/答案
36	建设工程监理概论	978-7-301-15518-9	曾庆军等	24.00	2009.9	ppt
37	◎地基与基础(第2版)	978-7-301-23304-7	肖明和等	42.00	2013.11	ppt/答案

序号	书 名	书 号	编著者	定价	出版时间	配套情况
38	地基与基础	978-7-301-16130-2	孙平平等	26.00	2010.10	ppt
39	地基与基础实训	978-7-301-23174-6	肖明和等	25.00	2013.10	ppt
40	土力学与地基基础	978-7-301-23675-8	叶火炎等	35.00	2014.1	ppt
41	土力学与基础工程	978-7-301-23590-4	宁培淋等	32.00	2014.1	ppt
42	土力学与地基基础	978-7-301-25525-4	陈东佐	45.00	2015.2	ppt/答案
43	建筑工程质量事故分析(第2版)	978-7-301-22467-0	郑文新	32.00	2013.9	ppt
44	建筑工程施工组织设计	978-7-301-18512-4	李源清	26.00	2011.2	ppt
45	建筑工程施工组织实训	978-7-301-18961-0	李源清	40.00	2011.6	ppt
46	建筑施工组织与进度控制	978-7-301-21223-3	张廷瑞	36.00	2012.9	ppt
47	建筑施工组织项目式教程	978-7-301-19901-5	杨红玉	44.00	2012.1	ppt/答案
48	钢筋混凝土工程施工与组织	978-7-301-19587-1	高 雁	32.00	2012.5	ppt
49	钢筋混凝土工程施工与组织实训指导(学生工作页)	978-7-301-21208-0	高 雁	20.00	2012.9	ppt
50	建筑施工工艺	978-7-301-24687-0	李源清等	49.50	2015.1	ppt/答案
		工程管理类				
1	建筑工程经济	978-7-301-24346-6	刘晓丽等	38.00	2014.7	ppt/答案
2	施工企业会计(第2版)	978-7-301-24434-0	辛艳红等	36.00	2014.7	ppt/答案
3	建筑工程项目管理(第2版)	978-7-301-26944-2	范红岩等	42.00	2016.3	ppt
4	建设工程项目管理(第二版)	978-7-301-24683-2	王 辉	36.00	2014.9	ppt
5	建设工程项目管理(第2版)	978-7-301-28235-9	冯松山等	45.00	2017.6	ppt
6	建筑施工组织与管理(第2版)	978-7-301-22149-5	翟丽旻等	43.00	2013.4	ppt/答案
7	建设工程合同管理	978-7-301-22612-4	刘庭江	46.00	2013.6	ppt/答案
8	建筑工程资料管理	978-7-301-17456-2	孙 刚等	36.00	2012.9	ppt
9	建筑工程招投标与合同管理	978-7-301-16802-8	程超胜	30.00	2012.9	ppt
10	工程招投标与合同管理实务	978-7-301-19035-7	杨甲奇等	48.00	2011.8	ppt
11	工程招投标与合同管理实务	978-7-301-19290-0	郑文新等	43.00	2011.8	ppt
12	建设工程招投标与合同管理实务	978-7-301-20404-7	杨云会等	42.00	2012.4	ppt/答案/习题
13	工程招投标与合同管理	978-7-301-17455-5	文新平	37.00	2012.9	ppt
14	工程项目招投标与合同管理(第2版)	978-7-301-24554-5	李洪军等	42.00	2014.8	ppt/答案
15	建筑工程商务标编制实训	978-7-301-20804-5	钟振宇	35.00	2012.7	ppt
17	建筑工程安全管理(第2版)	978-7-301-25480-6	宋 健等	42.00	2015.8	ppt/答案
18	施工项目质量与安全管理	978-7-301-21275-2	钟汉华	45.00	2012.10	ppt/答案
19	工程造价控制(第2版)	978-7-301-24594-1	斯 庆	32.00	2014.8	ppt/答案
20	工程造价管理(第二版)	978-7-301-27050-9	徐锡权等	44.00	2016.5	ppt
21	工程造价控制与管理	978-7-301-19366-2	胡新萍等	30.00	2011.11	ppt
22	建筑工程造价管理	978-7-301-20360-6	柴 琦等	27.00	2012.3	ppt
23	建筑工程造价管理	978-7-301-15517-2	李茂英等	24.00	2009.9	
24	工程造价案例分析	978-7-301-22985-9	甄 凤	30.00	2013.8	ppt
25	建设工程造价控制与管理	978-7-301-24273-5	胡芳珍等	38.00	2014.6	ppt/答案
26	◎建筑工程造价	978-7-301-21892-3	孙咏梅	40.00	2013.2	ppt
27	建筑工程计量与计价	978-7-301-26570-3	杨建林	46.00	2016.1	ppt
28	建筑工程计量与计价综合实训	978-7-301-23568-3	龚小兰	28.00	2014.1	
29	建筑工程估价	978-7-301-22802-9	张 英	43.00	2013.8	ppt
30	安装工程计量与计价(第3版)	978-7-301-24539-2	冯 钢等	54.00	2014.8	ppt
31	安装工程计量与计价综合实训	978-7-301-23294-1	成春燕	49.00	2013.10	素材
32	建筑安装工程计量与计价	978-7-301-26004-3	景巧玲等	56.00	2016.1	ppt
33	建筑安装工程计量与计价实训(第2版)	978-7-301-25683-1	景巧玲等	36.00	2015.7	
34	建筑水电安装工程计量与计价(第二版)	978-7-301-26329-7	陈连姝	51.00	2016.1	ppt
35	建筑与装饰装修工程工程量清单(第2版)	978-7-301-25753-1	翟丽旻等	36.00	2015.5	ppt
36	建筑工程清单编制	978-7-301-19387-7	叶晓容	24.00	2011.8	ppt
37	建设项目评估(第二版)	978-7-301-28708-8	高志云等	38.00	2017.9	ppt
38	钢筋工程清单编制	978-7-301-20114-5	贾莲英	36.00	2012.2	ppt
39	混凝土工程清单编制	978-7-301-20384-2	顾 娟	28.00	2012.5	ppt
40	建筑装饰工程预算(第2版)	978-7-301-25801-9	范菊雨	44.00	2015.7	ppt
41	建筑装饰工程计量与计价	978-7-301-20055-1	李茂英等	42.00	2012.2	ppt
42	建设工程安全监理	978-7-301-20802-1	沈万岳	28.00	2012.7	ppt
43	建筑工程安全技术与管理实务	978-7-301-21187-8	沈万岳	48.00	2012.9	ppt
44	工程造价管理(第2版)	978-7-301-28269-4	曾 浩等	38.00	2017.5	ppt/答案
		建筑设计类				
1	◎建筑室内空间历程	978-7-301-19338-9	张伟孝	53.00	2011.8	
2	建筑装饰CAD项目教程	978-7-301-20950-9	郭 慧	35.00	2013.1	ppt/素材
3	建筑设计基础	978-7-301-25961-0	周圆圆	42.00	2015.7	
4	室内设计基础	978-7-301-15613-1	李书青	32.00	2009.8	ppt

序号	书名	书号	编著者	定价	出版时间	配套情况
5	建筑装饰材料(第2版)	978-7-301-22356-7	焦 涛等	34.00	2013.5	ppt
6	设计构成	978-7-301-15504-2	戴碧锋	30.00	2009.8	ppt
7	基础色彩	978-7-301-16072-5	张 军	42.00	2010.4	
8	设计色彩	978-7-301-21211-0	龙黎黎	46.00	2012.9	ppt
9	设计素描	978-7-301-22391-8	司马金桃	29.00	2013.4	ppt
10	建筑素描表现与创意	978-7-301-15541-7	于修国	25.00	2009.8	
11	3ds Max 效果图制作	978-7-301-22870-8	刘 晗等	45.00	2013.7	ppt
12	3ds max 室内设计表现方法	978-7-301-17762-4	徐海军	32.00	2010.9	
13	Photoshop 效果图后期制作	978-7-301-16073-2	脱忠伟等	52.00	2011.1	素材
14	3ds Max & V-Ray建筑设计表现案例教程	978-7-301-25093-8	郑恩普	40.00	2014.12	
15	建筑表现技法	978-7-301-19216-0	张 峰	32.00	2011.8	ppt
16	建筑速写	978-7-301-20441-2	张 峰	30.00	2012.4	
17	建筑装饰设计	978-7-301-20022-3	杨丽君	36.00	2012.2	ppt/素材
18	装饰施工读图与识图	978-7-301-19991-6	杨丽君	33.00	2012.5	ppt
规划园林类							
1	居住区景观设计	978-7-301-20587-7	张群成	47.00	2012.5	ppt
2	居住区规划设计	978-7-301-21031-4	张 燕	48.00	2012.8	ppt
3	园林植物识别与应用	978-7-301-17485-2	潘利等	34.00	2012.9	ppt
4	园林工程施工组织管理	978-7-301-22364-2	潘利等	35.00	2013.4	ppt
5	园林景观计算机辅助设计	978-7-301-24500-2	于化强等	48.00	2014.8	ppt
6	建筑·园林·装饰设计初步	978-7-301-24575-0	王金贵	38.00	2014.10	ppt
房地产类							
1	房地产开发与经营(第2版)	978-7-301-23084-8	张建中等	33.00	2013.9	ppt/答案
2	房地产估价(第2版)	978-7-301-22945-3	张 勇等	35.00	2013.9	ppt/答案
3	房地产估价理论与实务	978-7-301-19327-3	褚菁晶	35.00	2011.8	ppt/答案
4	物业管理理论与实务	978-7-301-19354-9	裴艳慧	52.00	2011.9	ppt
5	房地产测绘	978-7-301-22747-3	唐春平	29.00	2013.7	ppt
6	房地产营销与策划	978-7-301-18731-9	应佐萍	42.00	2012.8	ppt
7	房地产投资分析与实务	978-7-301-24832-4	高志云	35.00	2014.9	ppt
8	物业管理实务	978-7-301-27163-6	胡大贝	44.00	2016.6	
9	房地产投资分析	978-7-301-27529-0	刘永胜	47.00	2016.9	ppt
市政与路桥							
1	市政工程施工图案例图集	978-7-301-24824-9	陈亿琳	43.00	2015.3	pdf
2	市政工程计价	978-7-301-22117-4	彭以舟等	39.00	2013.3	ppt
3	市政桥梁工程	978-7-301-16688-8	刘 江等	42.00	2010.8	ppt/素材
4	市政工程材料	978-7-301-22452-6	郑晓国	37.00	2013.5	ppt
5	道桥工程材料	978-7-301-21170-0	刘水林等	43.00	2012.9	ppt
6	路基路面工程	978-7-301-19299-3	偶昌宝等	34.00	2011.8	ppt/素材
7	道路工程技术	978-7-301-19363-1	刘 雨等	33.00	2011.12	ppt
8	城市道路设计与施工	978-7-301-21947-8	吴颖峰	39.00	2013.1	ppt
9	建筑给排水工程技术	978-7-301-25224-6	刘 芳等	46.00	2014.12	ppt
10	建筑给水排水工程	978-7-301-20047-6	叶巧云	38.00	2012.2	ppt
11	市政工程测量(含技能训练手册)	978-7-301-20474-0	刘宗波等	41.00	2012.5	ppt
12	公路工程任务承揽与合同管理	978-7-301-21133-5	邱 兰等	30.00	2012.9	ppt/答案
13	数字测图技术应用教程	978-7-301-20334-7	刘宗波	36.00	2012.8	ppt
14	数字测图技术	978-7-301-22656-8	赵 红	36.00	2013.6	ppt
15	数字测图技术实训指导	978-7-301-22679-7	赵 红	27.00	2013.6	ppt
16	水泵与水泵站技术	978-7-301-22510-3	刘振华	40.00	2013.5	ppt
17	道路工程测量(含技能训练手册)	978-7-301-21967-6	田树涛等	45.00	2013.2	ppt
18	道路工程识图与 AutoCAD	978-7-301-26210-8	王容玲等	35.00	2016.1	
交通运输类							
1	桥梁施工与维护	978-7-301-23834-9	梁 斌	50.00	2014.2	ppt
2	铁路轨道施工与维护	978-7-301-23524-9	梁 斌	36.00	2014.1	ppt
3	铁路轨道构造	978-7-301-23153-1	梁 斌	32.00	2013.10	ppt
4	城市公共交通运营管理	978-7-301-24108-0	张洪满	40.00	2014.5	ppt
5	城市轨道交通车站行车工作	978-7-301-24210-0	操 杰	31.00	2014.7	ppt
6	公路运输计划与调度实训教程	978-7-301-24503-3	高福军	31.00	2014.7	ppt/答案
建筑设备类							
1	建筑设备识图与施工工艺(第2版)(新规范)	978-7-301-25254-3	周业梅	44.00	2015.12	ppt
2	建筑施工机械	978-7-301-19365-5	吴志强	30.00	2011.10	
3	智能建筑环境设备自动化	978-7-301-21090-1	余志强	40.00	2012.8	ppt
4	流体力学及泵与风机	978-7-301-25279-6	王 宁等	35.00	2015.1	ppt/答案

注:🌐 为"互联网+"创新规划教材;★为"十二五"职业教育国家规划教材;◎为国家级、省级精品课程配套教材,省重点教材。相关教学资源如电子课件、习题答案、样书等可通过以下方式联系我们。

联系方式:010-62756290,010-62750667,85107933@qq.com,pup_6@163.com,欢迎来电咨询。